HERE WE GROW AGAIN

DEVOTIONS FOR SPIRITUAL GROWTH

Kyle Dodd

HERE WE GROW AGAIN

Library of Congress Cataloging-in-Publication Data

ISBN 1-887002-19-7
Dodd, Kyle
Kyle Dodd

Here We Grow Again / Kyle Dodd
Published by Cross Training Publishing, Grand Island, Nebraska 68803

Distributed in the United States and Canada by Cross Training Publishing

Cover Illustrator: Jeff Sharpton
Printed in the United States of America

For additional books and resources available through Cross Training Publishing contact us at:

Cross Training Publishing
P.O. Box 1541
Grand Island, NE 68802
(308) 384-5762

Kyle Dodd has been a keynote motivational speaker for: seminars, conferences, youth rallies and banquets for the past 16 years, speaking to youth and families on subjects such as peer pressure, sex and dating and parenting today's youth. If you would like to have Kyle as a speaker at a school function, youth club, FCA, church or any other event please call:

Kyle Dodd
Doulos Ministries Inc.
12550 Zuni Street
Westminster, CO 80234
Phone: 303 254-9278
Fax: 303 254-9195

Dedication

If it's okay with you, Reader, I'd like to dedicate this book and all the sleepless nights and long hours to *my* three disciples...my sons:

To Daniel—who melts our hearts.
To Dustin—who makes us laugh.
To Drew—who defines happiness.

"Her children rise up and bless her and her husband also." Proverbs 31:28

Acknowledgments

I'd like to recognize the following folks who provided the impetus for this book. If my thanks seem a little long winded...get over it...I am. First I'd like to say thanks to Gordon at Cross Training Publishing for believing in my dream when few did. To the sparkle in my eye, my wife Sharon, for taking up the slack when I didn't. To my couple's Bible study back in Branson for always being there when we needed them. Don't forget Rich, for showing me what "joy" looks like on two feet. Once again to my brothers, Coop, Bruce, and Joey for exemplifying what accountability means locking arms, and lastly, to my mentor/friend in heaven, Jimmy Greenwood...I miss ya' "Bean," and we'll go huntin' again when I get there. God, you are awesome!

Foreword

"I am a little pencil in the hand of a writing God who is sending a love letter to the world." Mother Teresa

Who has the last word? No doubt about it, God definitely has the last word! But, all of Kyle's friends (I'm so fortunate to be one of those) will tell you that Kyle has the next to the last word. He's fun, he's loony, he's creative, he's animated, he's easier'n a puppy to fall in love with, he talks a million miles a minute, but best of all, he has a raging heart for kids of all ages. Nothing makes him more excited than seeing young folks become ingrained in God's word and committed to the Savior who wrote it. Folks, one experience in this devotional book each day will put jet fuel in your spiritual pipes and fuel your fire with enthusiasm for the Creator of the paper it's written on.

Please heed this warning as you turn the page...if you should dare to read one of these devotions each day and commit your life to the truth shared, you had better prepare yourself for some drastic changes in your life. You're probably going to like what you see in the mirror a whole lot more, your face is probably going to smile a lot more than people around you are used to, and a surge of God's grace, peace, and forgiveness may just invade your soul for a lifetime. As Walt Disney said, "Get a good idea and stay with it. Dog it, and work at it until it's done, and done right." Reading this book daily is one of the best ideas that's come along in years.

Joe White, Ed. D

Table Of Contents

A BITTER THIEF

Forgiveness

"See to it that no one comes short of the grace of God; that no root of bitterness springing up causes trouble, and by it (bitterness) many be defiled." Hebrews 12:15

Recently I read something that stood out in my mind like a cowboy in London. The statement held that if *forgiveness* is the most therapeutic event in life, then *bitterness* must be the most destructive. I am amazed at the number of people today who seem to have a chip on their shoulder. I recall from my mental history book the time my sister purposely broke a model airplane that I had slaved a calendar year to build. I felt like blowing my top. Now, at the time of termination (my airplane's), I had a choice to make—either forgive and forget, or go ballistic and try out my new Ninja karate kick on my sister's Adam's apple.

This verse in Hebrews hits the nail on the head when it calls bitterness and anger what it really is—*trouble*. As you grow older you *will be* (not an option) mistreated, gossiped about, falsely accused, or taken advantage of. You'll have to deal with this abuse, whether mental or even physical, in a manner that solves, not adds to the problem. Your choices are to be ticked off and harbor (hold inside) the anger, or deal directly (using kind words) with the source. Let me clue you in...forgiveness is attainable only with divine power, not by mortal means. To actually forgive someone means to walk away and leave it for God to handle on His "to-do" list. No pay-backs, counter attacks, back-stabs, or revenge allowed in God's game. Just think of it this way: Jesus forgave you for all the times you broke his heart, so you should do the same for others, right? (Answer yes for bonus points!) Forgiveness feeds happiness and bitterness starves it.

Are you holding anger (bitterness) inside against anyone today? Can bitterness eat away at your joy like cancer? What can you do today, not tomorrow, to make things right with someone you harbor bitterness toward? Go do it!

THREE SIMPLE WORDS

Relationships

"Love never fails." 1 Corinthians 13:8
"Love covers a multitude of sins." 1 Peter 4:8

February 14 is Valentine's Day, a time set aside for lovers of all ages. This day for romanticism was created, no doubt, by florists, candy makers, and greeting card companies. Businesses rake in big-time cash simply by offering folks a creative way to say, "I love you," at that special time each year. Despite the hoop-la and commercialization, I think Valentine's Day is a great idea, and the male species needs all the help it can get. Perhaps you're asking yourself why I've included a devo on this event since you're probably reading it at a different time of year. Why? Because it is never too late or too early to tell someone you love them. Love is the high octane fuel that powers our engine and keeps us going. Relationships, whether with the opposite sex or not, need to be nurtured so they don't wither like a plant without water.

Unfortunately, millions of marriages, friendships, and working relationships are in trouble today because of the inability of those involved to get along. Maybe the fundamental problem is selfishness. We are so intent on satisfying our own needs and desires that we fail to recognize the longings of others. Relationships always work best when we think *less* about ourselves and more about another. True agape (unconditional) love is hardly a new concept. In fact, it's ancient. Jesus not only told us, He modeled for us, the way to develop, build, nurture, and sustain a valuable relationship. Whatever our height, weight, color, or shoe-size, we all have two basic needs—to love and be loved by someone. Begin today to humble yourself (even if you've been wronged) and mend an old relationship, work to maintain a current one, or develop a brand new relationship. Make Jesus the real cupid, a model for what it really takes, and what it really means to say three simple words—I...love...you!

What does love mean to you? Why is it so hard to maintain a relationship? How are you nurturing your relationships today?

Counsel

"Without consultation, plans are frustrated, but with many counselors they succeed." Proverbs 15:22

If I had one dollar for every piece of false counsel I've received in my lifetime, I'd single-handedly make Fort Knox go belly-up. Seeking guidance, direction, opinions, or advice on matters of importance in one's life can be a dangerous adventure. As you travel along life's journey of rock slides, sharp turns, steep grades, and uneven ground, you will value verbal road signs. Whether it's advice on a career change, marriage partner, financial investment, or simply a recommendation for a movie, you'll need direction. But be careful, when the *wrong* folks give counsel, it can cause real problems. Here is a quick lesson—most people who are wise enough to seek counsel from, *won't* give it until asked (and then they'll probably get back to you after some thought and prayer). Wise counsel is not the answer to every problem, but good, thought-provoking questions cause you to re-evaluate a situation and think through the process.

This information is probably not news to you. I do think that we all should be very selective of those we choose to guide and direct our decisions. Set up a "personal advisory board" made up of three people. The following is a check-list of qualifications for your board members:

Must be over forty years old.
Must be a Christian-Servant.
Must seek God *daily* through scripture study and prayer.
Must have at least one male and two females or two males and one female on the board.
Must have known you for at least five years .
Must use scripture based precepts as basis for counsel.

Use this group (board) as a sounding board for all your major decisions. Pray about who should be on your board, then call and ask them to participate. Good luck!

Ready to assemble a board? Who qualifies that you know? How can you go about asking them? What's the hold-up?

Relationships

"Be angry (what?) yet do not sin; do not let the sun go down on your anger." Ephesians 4:26

You know what? The older you become, the more you're gonna' realize how different and unique (Joke: How do you catch a unique rabbit? ...You neek up on it!) people really are. If you're lucky you'll realize just how unusual people think, act, believe, walk, and talk. In your search, you may also arrive at the brilliant conclusion that along with differences, conflict also seems to arise. And where conflict lives, you'll find strife as its neighbor. Strife resides next door to disharmony and anger. Now, after that boring little speech, I'd like to walk you through a way to solve the problem of anger and bitterness with a set of guidelines. These can be called, "The Twelve Ground Rules of Confrontation by Communication:"

Acknowledge your contribution to the problem.
Stick to today's problem and don't use the past as ammo (no "you always" or "you never" phrases).
Identify the real issue at hand, don't deal with the layers surrounding it.
Express your feelings and emotion with statements that begin with "I" instead of "you."
Avoid analyzing the other person's character (talk or behavior).
Avoid counter attacks and accept criticism graciously as a mature person.
Avoid "mind reading" what the other person means by a comment.
Keep short accounts (don't let the sun go down on your anger).
Maintain control of your tongue and emotions.
Don't attempt to win; seek mutually satisfying solutions to your disagreements.
No hitting below the belt (no cut-downs allowed).
When any of the above rules are broken, call a foul and get back on track.

If a problem should arise between you and anyone else, you *must* "get it right" with them soon. Remember, you don't make things right or resolve conflicts through gossip, letters, or denial—you do it by face-to-face communication. Good luck!

Who do you have anger toward today? When are you gonna' resolve it? Today?

MR. FIX-IT

Friendship

"Peter took Him (Jesus) aside and began to rebuke Him saying, 'God forbid it, Lord! This shall never happen to You.' He (Jesus) turned and said to Peter, 'Get behind Me, Satan! You are a stumbling block to Me; for you are not setting your mind on God's interests, but man's.'" Matthew 16:22-23

We've all been in old "Peppermint Socks'" shoes whenever we open our mouth and insert our pedal extremity (foot). Peter was no different than any one of us today. His sole desire in life was to be a friend and help out. The Savior first called Peter a rock, then four verses later tagged him as a stumbling block. Peter the rock turned into a rolling stone, tripping up those following the path of righteousness. Jesus described to His disciples the course necessary to fulfill His tour of duty on earth. The process included suffering, death, and the resurrection, but it just didn't compute for old Pete. He only heard (selective listening) the first two segments, and never got to the part of the story where Jesus would ride off into the sunset of eternity with the Father of the heavens.

I'll bet my bottom dollar that most of us have tried at one time or another to be a Mr. Fix-It and jump into what seemed like a broken area of a friend's life where God had initiated a remodeling project on some character flaws. The Creator is in the business of rebuilding broken homes and hearts. Suffering and rebuilding are part of the process, so you and I need only to encourage and pray for those who are being rebuilt. Jesus' response to Peter was harsh because He knew His Father's will for His life. Any barriers to that were considered evil.

So, the next time you see a friend or relative going through a tough time, determine if it's God doing some interior designing or the world doing some destroying. If it is of God, let it be. If it is of the world, jump in and help. The finished product will be in the next heavenly issue of *Better Homes.*

Why does God rebuild our lives? How can we know if we need to stay out of the way or help? What will your next response be to another person's trouble?

THERE IT BE

Following Christ

"Jesus said to His disciples, 'If anyone wishes to come after Me, let him deny himself, take up his cross and follow Me.'" Matthew 16:24

As a parent of three bouncing baby boys, I am amazed how natural it is for them to be selfish. It's like the first word out of their chirping mouths (even before "Mommy" or "Daddy") was *"mine."* That's right—these little guys didn't have to take a communication class or even learn the English language before they could bark out words of self. I guess (call me Big Daddy Clueless) I never realized what impact the sin of The Garden has on us today in terms of always focusing on ourselves. Is it any wonder, with only ten commandments escorted down Mt. Sinai by Moses, that one of them is, *"Love your neighbor as yourself?"* Just take a moment to reflect on how much we love ourselves. We're always checking ourselves out in the mirror, buying cool clothes, feeding our mouths on command, or otherwise indulging me, me, me.

Jesus had to remind His disciples over and over that to be His follower, they must *come to the end of self.* What Jesus asked of His twelve is asked of His followers today. I believe that Christ sits and waits at the end of the road called "Self." Jesus asks us to take up (carry) our own cross of suffering and ridicule and follow Him down the long road to Calvary. The times we sacrifice the old human nature and serve someone else will be the greatest joy we'll experience on this clump of dirt called Earth. Try it out. It will take all your strength, plus the intervention of God, but see how your self-image grows. See how many heads you'll turn when you deny yourself and go against all odds to show a wacked-out world just what a real Christian looks and acts like. Go ahead—try it. I promise you'll like it, and so will God.

Why is it so hard to be unselfish? What does it mean to you to "take up your cross" daily and follow Jesus? How can you be selfless today and make a huge difference in your world for Christ?

Discipleship

"No one can be my disciple who does not give up all his own possessions." Luke 14:33

It was one of those errand things that sent me into the jaws of the grocery store at rush hour. Granted, most men are banished from these "malls of meals" for the simple reason they haven't a clue what to buy, what aisle to search, or what has any nutritional value. My wife had endured one of those L...O...N...G days with the kids, so I thought (I always get into trouble when I start thinking) I would win the "Husband of the Month" award by volunteering to pick up a few items at the grocery store for her. My motive was good, but this chore would soon turn into a nightmare when I realized (*after* waiting through the check-out line) that I only had a twenty dollar bill and no checks with me. My calculator mind set immediately into action, figured up the cost of the items in my cart, and guess what? My total was $39.25, which by my calculations, left me in a real pickle of a position—and $19.25 short.

I'll never forget the humiliation as I stood there, trying to seek a quick line of credit in front of a mob of mad mothers. My problem wasn't necessarily bad shopping skills, as much as it was not counting the cost of my purchases. There are a lot of Christians walking around today doing what I did—not counting the entire cost of being a disciple of Christ. Jesus figured it up before He took on the job of Savior, and realized it would cost Him His life. In this passage of scripture, Jesus is explaining that a possession is anything that detours you from total commitment to Him. Don't get into the thick of this Christian stuff and *then* calculate the cost of being a *real* follower of Christ. Trust me—being short of the cost can bring on a whole lot of embarrassment.

How much has being a follower of Jesus cost you? What possessions must you give up to be a disciple? Why is Jesus so jealous of all our attention?

WHO BROKE THE BABY?

Abortion

"You shall not murder." Exodus 20:13

Well, well, let me think a minute...(that's long enough). Where, oh where have we seen or heard this little four word phrase before? I know! I know! It was when Moses scaled down that mountain called Sinai after his meeting with God-In-Person. He was carrying those tablets with the "Ten Suggestions" on them, right? Absolutely wrong, Pickle Lips! If your Bible reads the same as mine, I do believe they were called the "Ten Commandments," *not* suggestions. Herein lies the problem that we face today...folks don't respect, adhere, listen to, abide by, or follow these commandments, or worse yet, can't even identify these ten phrases of protection! I won't bore you with mind bloating statistics on our subject of discussion today—abortion. Help me out; clue me in; beam me up; do whatever tickles your fancy, but tell me how people get off on the idea that we have a "pro-choice" to eliminate human life? How and where did we develop the standard that if life inconveniences us, we play God and choose someone else's destiny. I mean, hey, the next time someone pulls out in front of you while you're driving, just pull out your trusty six-shootin' handgun and kill 'em! (Sound absurd? It is, but so is abortion.)

Forgive me for being on my soap box, but reader (you!), clue in and realize we are going "to hell in a hand basket" as a society. God commands us not to kill anyone, no how, no way, no one. Children are a gift from God no matter how they are conceived. I have a question. Is God all knowing? Does He know who is pregnant now (even if they don't) and who will be pregnant in their lifetime? Then why, even if someone becomes pregnant out of wedlock, do we think we, as a civilized (questionable) society, can *choose* someone else's destiny? Come on people, the choice is and always will be God's. Bombing clinics and killing doctors is *not* the solution to this problem—it's that people need a Savior and *you* need to tell them about yours. The right choice is God's choice.

Can you write down all Ten Commandments? Why do we have these guidelines? Will you memorize and live by them?

RIGHTS?

My Rights

"If thou wilt take the left hand, then I will go to the right; or if thou depart to the right hand, then I will go to the left." Genesis 13:9

Our society is big on rights as a nation. We hear it on the radio and TV talk shows, read it in the papers, listen to it in conversation—but what does it mean? We have the constitutional rights granted all United States citizens—free speech, a fair trial, freedom to worship whatever or whoever we wish, the right to bear arms (guns). My question is, do we have rights as followers of Jesus Christ? The answer is NO! As Christians (derived from scripture, not the world), we are now slaves, branches, sheep, children, ambassadors, and fishermen, all with a purpose. Our rights now become an extension of grace to live a life of love, joy, peace, abundance, fulfillment, and kindness, all with a final destination of eternity with God. They could be thought of more as privileges than rights.

As soon as you start to live a life of faith in God, a fascinating concept opens up before you, and the blessings are yours. You exercise the privilege to waive your rights and let God choose for you. God sometimes lets you get to a place of testing, a place where your own welfare would be the thing to consider if you weren't living a life of faith. When you are living by faith, you will joyfully waive your right to choose and leave it to God to decide what's best for you. Whenever your rights are made the guiding light in life, it dims your spiritual vision. You see, the great enemy of living life by faith in God is not sin, but the good which is not good enough. Good is always the enemy of *the best.* Waive your rights...all right?

What rights do you have as a follower of Christ? What rights do you have as a person apart from Christ? Do you exercise your rights or let God choose for you? Why or why not?

Trusting God

"Son of Man, can these bones live?" Ezekiel 37:3

Here is a question to get your brain churning. Can a twisted life be made right? Don't plod into a religious common sense answer and say, "Oh, yes, with a little more Bible reading and a few more prayers, it can be done." It's a ton easier and safer (we think) to *do* something than it is just to trust God. We often mistake panic for inspiration and that is why there are far more workers *for* Him than *with* Him. The degree of panic in action is equal to the degree of spiritual experience with God that is lacking. We are always trying to "fix it ourselves" instead of trusting that He has total control of the situation. There is such a big difference between my flesh and God's grace. Does this mean that I should sit on my buns and never try to help myself or others who are not right with God? Heck, no! It does mean that as I dive in, I make sure that I am not part of the problem, but part of the solution. We all have areas in our internal engines (lives) that need some tuning up by the master mechanic (God), so we need to trust Him and join Him as an assistant.

The purpose of this particular devo is not to stop you, but to direct you, as you continue your pursuit of Godliness. In other words, look before you leap, but after you look—make sure you leap.

What does it *really* mean to trust God? How have you trusted God lately? Do you have a tendency to trust yourself more than God? Why? How can you deepen your trust in Him today?

Trials

"Jesus answered, 'You know not what you ask. Are you able to drink of the cup that I shall drink and be baptized with the baptism that I am baptized with?' They said to him, 'We are able.'" Matthew 20:22

I have participated in sports all my life, and by doing so have found one practice necessary prior to any event—stretching. Come on now, we've all tried this ancient ritual to loosen up hamstrings as tight as guitar strings. Remember trying to touch your feet with a straight leg and feeling as if your arms had shortened or your legs had grown? I am still amazed at those flexible folks who can do the splits (ouch!) or even plant their face on the ground between their outstretched legs. These maneuvers are all designed to allow the person performing them an edge against injury and the opponent.

Throughout years of conducting job interviews, I've heard over and over again the same answer to this question. "Why do you want this job?" "I really want to be *stretched.*" Now, that answer may be well and good to land a job, but most folks don't know *everything* that it entails. Yes, we all want God to stretch us, but I've found we usually want it done *our* way and on *our* time schedule. In other words, we want perseverance without pain. We want growth without groans. We want maturity without madness. Realize that God sees areas in our lives that we hide even from ourselves and He performs surgery. Now, correct me if I'm wrong, but when a doc' goes to cuttin,' a patient has to have anesthesia to deaden the pain, otherwise it's gonna' hurt like a big dog. Yes, God will stretch your spiritual muscles to prepare you for the game of godliness. Okay? Now, count to ten and hold it!

Why do we need to be stretched? What causes us to pull spiritual muscles? Are you being stretched today? How?

SWORD OF MERCY

Word of God

"For the word of God is quick, and powerful, and sharper than any two-edged sword, piercing even to divide the soul and spirit, and of the joints and marrow, and is a discerner of the thoughts and intents of the heart." Hebrews 4:12

On February 24, 1995, my family and I found ourselves in London, England, for my brother-in-law's wedding. Needless to say, this old Texan felt a little out of place! If you were to ask me (doesn't matter—I'll give my opinion if you ask or not), I'd just as soon keep my big old size thirteen feet on good old American soil, but the in-law factor has a certain persuasiveness. Well, to make a long story longer, I figured if we *had to* be there, we should make the best of it and take a tour of the city. Believe-you-me, we saw it all, plus some. One of my favorite stops was the Tower of London. We got to see where some old king got tired of his wife and had her beheaded (obviously not while we were there). Besides heads rolling, we also saw the crown jewels of Queen Elizabeth and other British royalty.

One item that caught my eye was a sword called the "Sword of Mercy." It looked like all the other swords except that it had no pointed tip. Made total sense after I thought about it! A sword that showed mercy to its victim because without a point it couldn't kill them.

How Christians can learn from this! Are there times that we use God's word as a weapon, not to teach, but to destroy? Yes, the Bible is powerful, but do we use it to hurt instead of heal? Is our intent to tear down or rebuild? God has given us a weapon of truth to be used to fight the sin (Satan), not the sinner (person). Next time you pull out your sword to do battle, pull out the sword of mercy—Jesus did.

Why did God give us His word? How do you use it? Is your intent to help or hurt someone?

KILLER WEEDS

Bitterness

"See to it that no one comes short of the grace of God; that no root of bitterness springing up causes trouble, and by it many be defiled." Hebrews 12:15

It was hotter than chili peppers in mid-July. I would make a gentleman's wager that the soles on my sneakers were melting like butter on a hot frying pan. I had this idea (a real brainstorm) which was about as bright as a two-watt light bulb. How in the world I let my mom talk me and my dad into planting a garden is beyond my capacity to comprehend. I have a new-found respect for the farmers of America who actually enjoy this voyage of vegetation and can make an honest living at it. Now, if you've never had the pain...ah, I mean privilege of gathering groceries from the green earth, let my feeble mind take you through the process, one corn row at a time. Okay, I'll go real slow so I don't lose ya' along the way. First, you till the ground under. Second, you plant seeds of whatever your little heart desires to grow. Lastly, you water the little suckers. Now, was that tough? (You'll be tested on this Monday.) Oooh, yes, there is one small detail I forgot to tell you about: Weeds can grow up around your vegetables and choke them to death so all that's left are a few hard-as-rock peas.

Now, you must be asking yourself at this point, "Self, what the heck does a garden with weeds have to do with life?" Weeds are like bitterness that left unattended (and not dealt with) can grow up and choke out all the *life* in your life. There are lots of folks carrying around the excess baggage of bitterness. It robs all their joy and happiness like a slick shop-lifter. The way to deal with bitterness is as you would a weed—get to the root of the issue and pull it out. In other words, the best way to deal with it is *to deal with it!* Don't let your garden of life be overtaken with the worldliness of weeds. Communicate, deal with it, root it, and then walk away from it. Make sure you weed your life of bitterness on a daily basis so that you, in due time, will reap a good harvest.

What is bitterness? How does it spring up in your life? Do you have bitterness toward anyone today? How can you root it out of your life? Are you? When?

An End To A Means

God's Will

"Thy will be done on Earth as it is in heaven." Matthew 6:10

How many major decisions did you make last year? Better yet, how many decisions do you make each minute of your life? Perching on the fence of decision are issues like career moves, where to live, who to marry, what church to attend, or where to go to college. We can make hasty, emotional decisions, or we can let someone else make the call for us. Some demand a miraculous sign from heaven to confirm a decision, others postpone decisions indefinitely. Most decisions, I feel safe in saying, are not dictated by scripture, but brought on by pressure. Beware of making decisions based on restlessness or a desire to change. Carefully evaluate a decision that could cost you more in the long run than you can afford. Lastly, most decisions become obvious given enough time and information.

God has given us a means of guidance to help make decisions both big and small. Let's explore seven different means the Creator has supplied to help us discern His will:

The Bible (Folks read it for comfort but use Forbes *magazine for direction.)*
Prayer (It's the currency of our personal relationship with Christ.)
The Holy Spirit (He will never lead us in opposition to the written word of God.)
Our Conscience (It will be a more effective red light than a green one.)
Circumstances (Learn from them, don't analyze them.)
Counsel ("Plans fail for lack of counsel, but with many advisors they succeed." Proverbs 15:22)
Fasting (Do this occasionally and it will amount to nothing more than priming a rusty pump; do it regularly and it will be a gush of God's will.)

Knowing and finding the will of God for your daily life and future is not a Captain Hook buried treasure hunt. Hear this—God has a will for your life and He wants you to find it!

Do you have a clue what God's will is for your life? How do you seek His will? How can you use this as a tool to help you in the future?

Smoking

"I buffet my body and make it my slave, lest possibly, after I have preached to others, I myself should be disqualified." 1 Corinthians 9:27

I can't quite figure it out. Call me Boy Clueless, but is our society trying to snub out smoking, or cater to the coughing? Everywhere you look (and smell), cigarette smoking still catches the eye of fashion and the look of the luxurious. Now, maybe to some this devo is gonna' be as helpful as tennis shoes on ice, but maybe it could help just one of those who are hooked on this habit and need the incentive to quit. Well, honey, are you talkin' to the right guy! Let me impart to you just a few raving reasons why it's never too late to stop smoking.

After one day of not *smoking:*
Blood pressure levels will near normal
Blood oxygen will near normal
Carbon monoxide in blood will decrease drastically
Heart attack risk will decrease
After forty-eight hours:
Nerve endings begin to re-grow
Sense of smell and taste improve
After two weeks to three months:
Circulation improves
Exercise becomes easier
Lung function increases thirty-percent
After one year:
Risk of heart attack falls by fifty-percent
After five years:
Stroke risk reduced
Reduced risk of several types of cancer
After ten years
Pre-cancerous cells will have been replaced by the body
After fifteen years
Risk of coronary disease same as non-smoker

Come on now Slick, take another gander at those stats. Correct me if you dare, but I have a faint feeling that God didn't intend for us to smoke these cancer sticks. If you don't smoke, don't start. If you do, stop! This world has enough natural hazards to survive, let alone creating our own.

Why do you think our bodies are a temple of God? Think about how important is it to view our bodies as Christ's condo. Do you do anything that harms your body?

Friendship

"Jonathan was knit to the soul of David, and Jonathan loved him (David) as himself." 1 Samuel 18:1

It makes our lives happier, improves our daily productivity, boosts our confidence level and self-worth, and most importantly, strengthens our walk with God. This endangered species in the wilderness of words is intimacy, or *into-me-see.* Intimacy is the ability to experience an open, supportive, compassionate relationship with another person without fear of condemnation or loss of individual identity. Men seem to struggle most with this lost art to masculinity while women appear to come by it naturally (there are exceptions to both). Men need to be more like Esau, who grieved when he lost his birthright. David mourned the death of his blood covenant friend, Jonathan, whom he loved like a relative. Women, this devo is targeted at encouraging men to dive into the unknown and unlikely—to begin the pursuit of quality relationships with men in an accountable scriptural fashion.

To put it in clear form, I will list the five levels of a relationship, then follow them with barriers to intimacy:

Level 1 is talking about the weather or other vague subjects.

Level 2 is offering an opinion about the weather.

Level 3 is expressing a belief or conviction.

Level 4 is when others share their dreams, fears, and emotions with me.

Level 5 is when I share my dreams, fears, and emotions with others.

Note: Many men can get to Level 3, but *true* relationships take place on Levels 4 and 5.

Barriers for men:

Men don't give each other affection.

Men don't nurture each other.

Men don't talk to each other about intimate things.

Men don't befriend other men just to enjoy their friendship.

Listen up! Before you dive into this unnatural episode you should know that this formula leads to intimacy and includes solid identity, empathy, loyalty, basic trust, and delay of gratification. Do yourself a favor and realize that with this type of relationship you'll become vulnerable and Christ-like.

What does intimacy mean to you? Is your answer sexual? Why is friendship's worldly definition wrong?

Shoulder To Shoulder

Fellowship

"It is not good for man to be alone." Genesis 2:18

For African President Nelson Mandela and his prison mates, keeping dignity intact required shared vision, commitment to bear one another's burdens, and strength to stand in unity no matter what the opposition. In *Time* magazine (November 28, 1994) Mandela wrote, "The authorities' greatest mistake was keeping us together, for together our determination was reinforced. It would be very hard, if not impossible, for one man alone to resist. I do not know if I could have done it had I been alone. Whatever we learned, we shared, and by sharing we multiplied whatever courage we had individually. The stronger ones raised up the weaker ones and both became strong in the process."

What a powerful story, don't you think? I mean, here is a guy who was in the "Gray Bar Hotel" (prison) and now answers to the code name "Hey, Pres'." What a tremendous lesson (and one we can learn without taking up residence in the pen) about staying shoulder to shoulder with other Christians in the midst of adversity. If God wanted us to be loners all our lives and have no fellowship, I think He would have put us each on our own personal planet to sit and rotate on our axis all our lonely life. A ton of strength lies in those "friends that stick closer than any brother." Don't be fearful that it may take some time to develop a shoulder to shoulder relationship with someone. Don't put off until tomorrow what can help you today. Don't make yourself out to be some super hero with an emblem on your chest. Don't be a cowboy (or girl) riding into the sunset alone, acting all tough. Don't you hate reading the word "don't" ten times straight? Okay, then just do it!

Write down a list of your top ten best friends (I'll wait). Okay, now which ones of these folks do you stand shoulder to shoulder with? Why or why not? How can you develop this today?

JESUS THE C.E.O.

Person of Christ

"In everything you do put God first and He will direct you and crown your efforts with success." Proverbs 3:6

Okay, here's a wacked-out thought for you to compute in your cranium. Can you imagine if Jesus came back to earth today dressed not in a cloak and sandals, but in pin-stripes and Cole-Haans? What if He drove a Lexus downtown to a sizable skyscraper and took over as "the boss" (Chief Executive Officer) of a major investment firm on Wall Street? Could He succeed? Let's just see...in only three short years Jesus defined a mission and formed strategies to carry it out to completion. He had a small staff of twelve unlikely, unqualified, unruly disciples. With that staff He organized Christianity, which today has branches in all corners of the world and a 32.4 % share of the population—twice the size of the closest rival's. His salesmen (disciples) took all they learned and utilized it in everyday life. Jesus (the marketing master) developed original material to market eternity to a broad-based region of purchasers. His salesmen learned sizzlin' sales-pitches like salvation, love, joy, healing, heaven, and guaranteed success.

I think it would be interesting to compare today's tycoons' self-help strategies with Christ's divine one-liners. Catch this idea—if people in the corporate world would review the real book of success (the Bible), I think they might learn something. (Scripture is, was, and always will be a landmark for you and I, no matter what career path we choose.) Don't slough off that thick, dusty, unused book on the piano (the Bible) as just a fable of fiction, value it as words of wisdom. Jesus' way to climb the corporate ladder will surprise you—it's by goin' down it.

Ask your father (or any business man) what his secret to success is, then compare that with Matthew 5:1-10.

Following In My Father's Paw Prints

God's Will

"Many are the plans (future) in a man's heart, but the counsel of the Lord will stand." Proverbs 19:21

From the magnificent musical opening and breath-taking African vistas, to the rip-roaring, (pun...get it?), emotionally charged climax, *The Lion King* movie reigns as animation's supreme champion. Set in the majestic beauty of the Serengeti, Disney's epic tells the heart warming story of the love between a proud lion ruler, Mufasa, and his young son, Simba—a curious cub who "just can't wait to be king." Out from the darkness crawls Simba's jealous Uncle Scar and his hyena hit-men. Their scheming for the throne leads to the tragedy of death for Mufasa, and Simba is exiled from the kingdom he should rightfully rule. Befriended by the warmhearted warthog, Pumbaa and his maniac meerkat friend, Timon, Simba forgets his responsibilities and adopts the carefree lifestyle of "Hakuna Matata" (means: don't worry). Rafiki, the wise and mysterious baboon, helps Simba reclaim his territory and eventually his position as King, just like his father.

This devo is targeted mainly at the male species who roam this jungle of society searching for prey...the future. This is one devo I feel I am qualified (somewhat) to write. I grew up with a huge desire to follow in my father's footsteps (paw prints). Males often don't realize until later on in life what an influence their fathers can have on them. God (our true Father) has a specific, hand-picked, custom designed plan for our lives and future. There is nothing wrong with wanting to do as your dad, but don't be disappointed (or surprised) if God's way points another direction. Some reading this may very well take up where their dad left off...but remember, no one is a failure if God leads them to a different destination. Always remember to enjoy and learn along life's journey until coming face to face with our Savior in eternity. Keep on prowling!

What does (did) your father do for a living? Do you see yourself following his footsteps? Why or why not? What if God's plans are different than your father's? Is that okay? Are you sure?

Finding The Real Me

Who I Am In Christ

"But we all, with unveiled face beholding as in a mirror the glory of the Lord are being transformed into the same image from glory to glory just as from the Lord, the Spirit." 2 Corinthians 3:18

Every time I pick up a magazine or scan the bookstore shelves these days, I find several publications that *try* (key word in sentence) to decipher the "real" me.

It appears we all give ourselves away psychologically every time we choose Pepsi over Coke or eat cold Wheaties instead of hot Cream of Wheat. One article I read counseled me on how the colors I choose could tell me what sort of mood I was going to be in that day (go figure). Never mind wasting all that time in a shrink's office on a couch, just let someone interpret your wardrobe. I never clued in that maybe wearing a red T-shirt could strip my emotions bare to the world...awesome dude! On one of those classy (yeah, right) talk shows the other day, they had as the guest a "mood evaluator" who told the audience you can give your life-long secrets away by what you wear, drive, buy, or sell (sounds a little "iffy" to me).

I'm not so sure that this practice of "finding one's self" isn't an age old tradition. The ironic thing is that the book *I've* been reading (the Bible) tells me to "deny self" in order to find it...get it? You know....lose to find, die to live, bury to resurrect? Wait a minute—this thinking goes against every concept or theory known to modern man. You will not, I repeat, will not find the "real you" until you get rid of self for the cause of Christ. The "real you," by nature (the sin one), has the capability to murder, lie, cheat, steal, hate, boast...need I go on? The Christ in you, after you remove self and replace it with Him, has the capacity to experience real peace, love an enemy, have compassion for the hungry, and forgive the unforgivable. Sound like you? No, because it's not the "real you," it's the "transformed you." Now that's one transformation even the crew of the Starship Enterprise couldn't figure out.

What is it that makes us want to find (like it's hiding) the "real me?" Why do you think Jesus wants us to die to self? Why is that process so hard? How can you deny yourself in the next hour? Go do it, okay?

A PROCESS

God's Will

"This is the will of God that by doing right you may silence the ignorance of foolish men." 1 Peter 2:15

I had a friend who once said, "There is nothing more dangerous than becoming comfortable out of God's will." Wow! Now, that's a truth you can hang your hat on. This devo is a custom designed formula to help determine God's will for *you* in the big decisions for your life. This formula is practical and simple. Before beginning you must let go of (ditch it!) your own will and sincerely desire God's will for your life. Otherwise, this process is about as helpful as a screen door on a submarine. Each step will build on itself and you may find the answer is obvious before you get to the end. If it doesn't make itself clear, keep moving through the steps until it does.

Step 1. Write down the decision you're trying to make. Nothing clarifies thinking more quickly than paper and pencil, because half the decision is knowing the problem. What are the choices?

Step 2. Write out a statement of purpose that explains why you are considering this decision. Why do you need to decide? What is the content (meat) of this decision? Are you unhappy? Is this a *need* or a *want*?

Step 3. Submit your statement of purpose to a series of questions. What are you trying to accomplish and why? What are your expectations? What would Jesus do? Is it a sense of calling or duty?

Step 4. If your answer isn't obvious, list all your options on a separate sheet—left side, pros (good), right side, cons (bad).

Step 5. If the answer still isn't clear, then...wait! Never push God. He is in a different time frame. He may use the time to work something into or out of *your* character. Note: God is not the author of confusion, Satan is! Peace is the umpire in this game.

Hey, this is one of many ways to search out God's clear pathway in the midst of a fog. Ask Him to open your spiritual eyes and show you the way...trust me, it's the *only* way!

Do you have a major decision on the horizon? What are you doing about it now? Is it important to you to be in God's will?

Communion

Cleansing

"Do this in remembrance of me." Luke 22:19

When was the last time you took communion? Do you know what this ritual of righteousness (and just plain getting right) with God means? What does it mean to drink and eat of the body of Christ? What do the wine (juice) and bread symbolize?

These are all great questions with valid answers. Communion should be a regular occurrence in our lives as followers of Christ. I'm going to share an illustration I heard once that explains what communion is all about. A few years ago the father of a family died from a sudden heart attack. The mother decided not to take their two young children to the funeral. She thought it would be too hard for the children to see their father being put in the ground. Years later, the cemetery remained a fearful place for them. Six years after the funeral, a friend of the family invited them all to go see the grave and read what was inscribed on the tombstone. It read, "Here lies a kind and gentle man." The friend brought along a basket of food in hopes they could have a picnic near the grave. At first it seemed a strange idea to the family, but they consented. After the event, the kids lost their fear of the cemetery forever.

Isn't this similar to what Jesus told his disciples to do when He asked them to share bread and wine in memory of Him? Wasn't the tomb that Jesus was buried in empty now? Isn't remembering His death and resurrection more of a celebration than a time of sorrow? Communion is a celebration of remembrance. It's a time of renewal and redemption that cleanses our mistakes and draws us from the death of sin to victory in Christ. Next time you take communion, enter into the holiness of God and ask for pardon. Prepare for victory as you eat and drink of Christ's cup.

When did you last take communion? How often do you take it? Is it just a rehearsed ritual or an awesome attitude?

The Mask

Who I Am In Christ

"For I am confident in this very thing, that He who began a good work in you will perfect it until the day of Christ." Philippians 1:6

"SSSmokin'!"..."Somebody stop me!"...In the block-buster movie, *The Mask,* when Stanley (actor Jim Carey) finds an ancient mask under a bridge, he believes his luck is finally going to change. By putting on the mask he is transformed into an indestructible, wise-cracking, smart-talking hero who fights the mob to save his girl. This comedy is full of one-liners, animation, and plenty of gut-bustin' laughs. The story line, in a nutshell, is that when the mask is worn, the innermost desires come to the surface. In other words, if the wearer is a good person, the mask enhances those qualities, but also does the same for a bad person.

How many folks do you know who wake up with one mask, but wear another when they leave the house? How about you? We live in a self-fulfilling, self-satisfying, self-fish (get it?) world of people-pleasers. We are constantly trying to be accepted, not rejected, fit in, not fade out, set the pace, not fall from grace. It seems like all that junior high peer pressure would wear out by the time we get to college. Let me clue you in...it doesn't get easier as it goes. The one and only reason folks masquerade in a custom-fitted mask is the "fear" (broad term) of rejection from peers (fancy, over-used word for friends). In our ruthless social circles we de-friend, de-file, and de-face those who de-fy the rules and stand confident of who they are. The common thread that runs through all those who are socially secure, is Christ. We won't be satisfied, stable, unselfish, or secure unless divine intervention occurs. The ending to the movie is a great shot of Stanley throwing his mask off a bridge and being accepted for who he really is...fearfully and wonderfully made. Clothes, diets, sports, cars, jobs, dates, or hair-do's don't make a person—only Jesus does that, and He did it in His biography called *The Bible.* Read it sometime. It receives rave reviews.

Why do people wear masks? Do you wear one? If you do, why? If you don't, why don't you? If you are wearing one now, how can you get rid of it?

Free For All

Freedom In Christ

"It was for freedom that Christ set us free, therefore keep standing firm and do not be subject again to the joke of slavery." Galatians 5:1

The big city can be one of the most happenin' places on the planet. In my years of travel, I have had a blast mixing with millions and loving the lights. Those cosmos of confusion can get on your nerves after a while though. Recently, on a trip to London I realized that in a city of eight million weird people, cabbies, discos, theater districts, subway rides, concrete buildings, and nerve racking noise levels, I needed some relief. My relief came not from an aspirin, but from a jog in beautiful Hyde Park. The feeling of satisfaction was not necessarily from the jog (I run like a pregnant elephant), but from the sheer fact that in the midst of metroplex madness, I found freedom in the wide open spaces of a luxury landscape. There were all shapes, colors, and sizes of pedestrians roller-blading, feeding the ducks, flying kites, baggin' rays, pushing strollers, swinging, throwing Frisbees, and just plain chillin' out with a friend on the lush green grass. It was a real free-for-all for anyone who wished to partake (free of charge, too!). It was like one minute I was in the city, the next minute in the country, and the line that separated the two was a single street.

What a neat lesson! I learned that in the midst of madness (this busy world) I can still find a refuge in the park (God's presence) and the price and reward for both are the same...freedom. We all need to take a daily break from our treadmill lives and find time to sit down with God in a park (or any quiet spot), early in the morning or late at night. You may not think it's important, but it's essential for your sanity and spiritual survival. Being a growing, thriving, excited follower of Christ can be as easy as a walk in the park...it's freeing-for-all who take it.

Are you entangled in your daily routine? How do you cope with it? Where does God fit into your schedule each week? How can you fit Him in more often? Then do it!

Evolution

"For by Him all things were created, both in the heavens and on earth, visible and invisible, whether thrones or dominions or rulers or authorities—all things have been created by Him and for Him. Colossians 1:16

Let's see how well you listened in your history class. I'll give you some clues and you give it a guess. He (obviously not a female) was born in 1809 and died at the age of seventy-three in 1882. At the age of twenty-two he was about to pursue a career working in the church, but decided at the last minute to take an offer as a naturalist (whatever that is) on a survey ship called the H.M.S. Beagle in 1831. He traveled abroad collecting organisms from all the major continents and returned to England to sort through his findings in 1836. For twenty years at his home in Kent, he dissected his thoughts, theories, and material, finally publishing a book in 1859 entitled *Origin of the Species* which supported his theory of evolution. Who was this man? (Give up yet?)

He was Charles Darwin, a man who impacted and influenced history as much as any one man ever has. His theory, which I'm not sure was ever meant to be considered factual, was and is a major influence in the debate of where we come from...God or monkeys. Now you might be wondering why I'm making such a big tiff about this man. Why...? Because if his theory is true, then you and I have no higher authority, no Savior, and surely no hope but to evolve into bones in the dirt. All who have grown up in a public school have been pounded with this theory. If you are told something enough, you may eventually believe it as truth. I'll tell you what this theory is in four words: a big fat lie. You, me, and whoever will be, are created by the Creator (Abba Father) and our family tree doesn't have apes hanging on it. Evolution is a joke and creation is the fact...learn it, live it, and believe it.

How come Darwin's theory is a theory, not a proven fact? If it is only a theory, then why do we believe it and teach it as fact? What can you do to transform your thinking?

Scarred For Life

Being a Christian

"You have been bought with a price, don't be the servants of man." 1 Corinthians 7:23

If you're ever doing the "traveling thing" and your journey happens to take you across the western plains of Texas, you'll see tumbleweeds, windmills, miles of pasture, fields of bluebells, old post-card gas stations, and the state bird of Texas—the cow. That's right, there are more of those lonesome doggies (cows) per square mile in the area around Hereford, Texas, than anywhere else in the world. You'll find every make of cow imaginable from Black Angus to the white-faced Hereford. In the late 1800's the cattle industry experienced a surge in what they commonly called, "cattle rustlin,'" which was really just plain stealing. The thieves rustled up someone else's herd and took it to market to sell for themselves. With so many large herds of cattle coming in each day, it was difficult to identify one rancher's cow from the next. Little could be done to stop the thieves unless they were caught red-handed. That was true until the invention of the "branding iron," which permanently marked livestock with the custom brand of the owner's ranch name, like JH, T-Bar-M, or Bar-K.

Believe it or not, you, as a follower of Christ, have been branded (spiritually, not physically). Remember that the brand symbolizes ownership and loyalty to a particular person and place of residence. As a Christian your owner (Jesus) paid the debt on the cross and now your future pasture of peace is heaven. Isn't that cool, to think you are scarred with the mental brand of Calvary, setting you apart from the others you rub shoulders with every day? Be proud of your owner, yet humble to your position here on earth. The hot branding iron process that marked the rawhide of a cow was a painful procedure, but your pain was borne by your Savior. What a deal!

What does being bought with a price say about Christ's love for you? Are you proud to be a member of the heavenly herd? How can you help others know about your future pasture?

I Do

Marriage

"For this cause a man shall leave his father and mother and cleave (marry) to his wife; and they shall become one flesh." Genesis 2:24

Call it matrimony, wedlock, affiliate, unite, bond, get hitched, lockin' up or whatever, but it all equates to marriage. The dictionary defines marriage as, "(mar' ij) the state of being married (well, duh?), a legal contract entered into by a man and a woman (what do gays think of this?) to live together as husband and wife." In the good old USA we seem to have reduced marriage to more of a "do it till it won't work anymore" mentality. Six to seven out of ten marriages today end up in divorce court settling issues of custody, alimony, and possessions. Take a second and read carefully what you will say during your wedding, "I *(fill in your name)* do take *(fill in spouse's name)* to be my wedded husband/wife, to have and to hold from this day forward, for better or worse, for richer or poorer, in sickness and in health, to love and to cherish, for as long as we both shall live, and to this I pledge you my love."

Granted, you're probably not at the point or age yet to be playin' on this field, but look at what is being promised (committed) here. If and when you are blessed (by God) to take this oath of unity, you need to realize these aren't just elegant words, but words of promise. Maybe you (as I do) come from a family that has lived through the parents breaking their vows of marriage and getting a divorce. Let me clue you in...you *don't* have to follow that same pattern of broken promises or empty love. For whatever reason, divorce is considered normal, acceptable, and okay by our society, but not by our Savior (Jesus). Begin now to realize how indescribable the institution of marriage is and how important it is to take it as a serious, life-long (one of the vows) agreement. Make your "I do" a promise and not a hidden "I may." Marriage will be the toughest thing you'll ever love.

Will you get married someday? Describe your future mate? Visualize what you think they'll look like. Do you see yourself celebrating a sixty year anniversary? If not, then forget it!

GUILTY OR NOT GUILTY

Saved By Grace

"But because of his great love for us, God, who is rich in mercy, made us alive with Christ even when we were dead in transgressions—it is by Christ you have been saved.." Ephesians 2:4-5

Seen by millions as a media obsession, it was impossible to flip through the channels without finding an update of the most recent events. Society was addicted to the case; conversations filled with speculation. Coverage of the O.J. Simpson trial dominated nightly news and check-out line tabloids. This case became the cultural phenomenon of the century. I got caught up in the intensity of the interrogations as attorneys Marsha Clark and Johnny Cochran went head to head, combating with literary clichés and courtroom jargon. We all knew O.J.'s past college football stardom at U.S.C. and celebrated professional career. Who could ever convince a jury to believe that such terrible charges could be justified against one so widely admired? In every sense of the phrase, "the jury was still out," until the verdict was released.

The great theologian, John Calvin, wrote brilliantly about the "total depravity of man," charging that within us all resides the capability or propensity (what a big word) to commit horrible acts. Until we realize our need for a Savior, it is difficult to get very excited about the work that Jesus accomplished on Calvary's cross two thousand years ago. It is against the ugly, black, and despairing backdrop of our own capacity for evil that the offer of God's marvelous grace shines like the crown jewels. In some sense, the O.J. Simpson trial forced us to ask deeper questions about ourselves and our own condition. Could O.J. have done it? Maybe we asked the wrong question...think about it? Without Christ anyone has the capability.

How is it that evil prevails? Who invented evil? Are you personally capable of committing evil? How do you prevent it? Is it important to you to spend daily time with Jesus? Do you? Why or why not?

Leadership

"Follow me and I will make you fishers of men." Matthew 4:19

In a world that thrives on *new* styles, techniques, technology, theories, and processes, we tend (at times) to drift away from basic truths. We don't have to walk too far to see how this culture defines leadership and the style that accompanies it. We are surrounded, like flies at a summer picnic, by people wanting to lead without a clue. They dictate, dominate, mandate, and accumulate a leadership style contradictory to that which Christ modeled some two-thousand years ago. Catch this idea...you can't be an effective leader until you become a humble follower (of Christ). The best style I've seen is not being the head of the class, but by bringing up the rear. Effective leadership is not the most enviable position on the planet. You'll be pulverized, criticized, and analyzed as long as you hold that particular seat of office. Everyone wants to get there, but few want to pay the price of admission.

For some unforeseen reason, God has placed me in a role of leading others. I have failed more than I have succeeded, but one thing I learned quickly...you don't do it by bossin' others around. You do it by modeling (showing) to others by your speech, actions, and re-actions. You don't just arrive as a leader, it's a process of trial and error. There are few ministries, corporations, or teams that are being lead by a Godly leader. You, yes little ol' you, can be the leader you were meant to be if you use God's formula to come up with the answers. Remember, this type of leadership won't go out of style.

Do you think you have the capability to be an effective leader? Who is the best leader you know? What makes them so good? Write down the qualities of an effective leader and see how they jive with scripture?

PRACTICING "SAFE" SEX

Sex

"Let marriage be held in honor among all, and let the marriage bed be undefiled; for fornicators and adulterers God will judge." Hebrews 13:4

Talk about a catchy ad. This one showed up in the University of Missouri school paper on February 14, 1995. The caption was, "Practice Safe Sex," and the picture, which spoke loudly, was a married couple walking down the aisle in the tux and wedding dress. Waiting until one is married to have sexual relations (they're kidding, right?) is a message that can't be stressed enough in our generation. Whether we like it or not, sex is more than just a handshake. It is more physiologically, psychologically, emotionally, and spiritually, than we make it out to be. Sexuality is a gift from God that is ours to share with someone in our future married life. Sex is not dirty, evil, or wrong. To the contrary, it is wonderful and miraculous. Sex is the most intimate, deepest part of ourselves, but our sexuality can become unsatisfying and unfulfilling if we use it inappropriately.

It is important to understand that sex will always *seem* appropriate and necessarily good because it is a desire we possess so deeply as human and spiritual beings. We all desire to commune with one another yet we go about it wrong. Although the present can be passionately deceiving, it is always the case that sex outside a lifelong, monogamous, committed relationship (marriage) is ultimately unfulfilling beyond physical arousal and release. Many, unfortunately, have learned this lesson the hard way. Those who lost their virginity prior to marriage often look back in wonder at something meaningless and empty that seemed "right" at the time. It's *always* worth the wait. Sex within the parameters mentioned above *will* be exponentially and unequivocally more wonderful and secure than one could ever dream. Practice "safe sex" and wait until you're married.

Why is it so hard to wait? Why don't so many wait? Are you willing to see beyond the passion and wait until you're married? Why is virginity the best wedding gift you could ever give your mate?

Nose To Nose

Confrontation

"Faithful are the wounds of a friend, but deceitful are the kisses of an enemy." Psalms 27:6

Why doesn't everyone think like you? Why did God have to create so many, so differently? As the gray hair begins to sprout on your head like daisies in a field, you'll realize how difficult it is to get along well with people. Whether at work, on a team, in a club, or even in the midst of your own family, you'll always find conflicts in interests and beliefs. The problem rears its ugly head when we don't handle differences as God intended. Violence and anger seem to be popular means of dealing with differences. Why? Because we don't realize that difference can be the sharp tool God uses to chip away character flaws. Think about it, confrontation has a way of bringing out both the best and the worst in us.

Our society seems to have lost the meaning of friendship. We label as friends those who are really only acquaintances. A real friend is someone for whom you would lay down your life. A friend is someone who sticks closer than a blood relative through the highs and lows. A friend loves enough to point out flaws in our character in order to make us better. A friend warns us of upcoming dangers and hazards we may soon encounter. A friend loves at all times. Don't be afraid to point out, not judge, a friend's weaknesses that are inhibiting a fulfilling life with Christ. Don't knit-pick issues that don't matter, choose what mountains to climb with a friend and go for it. Deal with issues that go against scripture. To love a friend, you'll have to learn to be one first!

What is your definition of friendship? Are you a real friend? What could make you a better friend? Ask a friend what you could do to be a better friend.

Faith

"Faith is the assurance of things hoped for, the conviction of things not seen." Hebrews 11:1

Talk about a racket! It wasn't like I had a whole lot of choice in the matter—either Ryder or U-Haul. We were moving from the world's largest parking lot, Branson, Missouri, to the Mile High City of Denver, Colorado. It was 826 miles cross-country to the Rockies *and* we had to cross Kansas (boring). We (mostly my wife) packed boxes for about six weeks prior and still it seemed we had a ton to do. Our local Bible study group was a huge help and without them we still wouldn't be moved. The night before the drive, my exhausted wife and I sat amid our crashed-out kids, staring at the shell of a home. We were really gonna' miss our friends, yet the excitement and anticipation was fun.

There's something unnerving about packing up and moving to an unfamiliar destination. It reminds me of packing up for the first year of college and moving into the athletic dorm at Oklahoma University. All so different, uncertain what to expect around the next corner—new home, new friends, new schools, new church, new roads, new scenery. Like the Mayflower's maiden voyage into uncharted seas, faith is all about the unseen and uncertain. God asks us every day to set sail into waters never crossed before...do something that we've never done, speak when we've never spoken, share when we don't know how. Jesus didn't let the grass grow under His or His disciples' feet. So, next time God transplants you in some unfamiliar place, realize that you'll grow where you're planted because He goes too. Bon voyage!

Why is it so hard to accept change? Do you see how change draws you close to God and increases your faith in Him?

Wine Press

Trials

"I now rejoice in my sufferings for you, and fill up that which is behind of the afflictions of Christ in my flesh for His body's sake." Colossians 1:24

We continually strive for those mountain top experiences of life. Prior to conversion to Christ, you may have lived daily on the top, yet after this experience you learn a revolutionary lesson. God can allow life with Him to rivet us with pain that is more intense than anything we might have dreamed. One moment we are lost, then after a radiant flash, we see what He is really after and say, "Lord, here I am. Do what needs doing to make me more like you." This event has nothing to do with personal sanctification, but instead being made broken bread and poured-out wine. God can never make us into wine if we object to the fingers He uses to squeeze the grapes (you and me). If God would only use His own fingers we would feel special. But when He uses someone we don't like or a set of difficult circumstances as the crushers, we hate it. We must never choose our own martyrdom (pain). If we want to be made into wine, we *will* be crushed because no one can drink grapes. Grapes only become wine when they're crushed.

If by chance the grapes of your spiritual walk are not ripe, then the wine would be bitter if God squeezed you. You have to be totally in tune with God before the squeezing and pouring out process can take place. Keep your life "right" with God and let Him have His way with you and you will see that He is producing the kind of bread and wine that will benefit His Kingdom. The older you get the sweeter the wine will become in life...you'll see.

What kind of finger and thumb of God has been squeezing you? Why is pressure so important on the wine press? If you're not getting squeezed, then what do you see as the problem? When will you be ready?

Turf Talk

Accountability

"Keep fervent in your love for one another, because love covers a multitude of sins." 1 Peter 4:8

You hear the word "turf" used a lot when describing a field for athletic competition. In this case, I want to talk from a different perspective. I would like to use "turf" as meaning common ground, not a playing field. As you grow older, you will notice more and more how creative our Creator was (and still is) in designing humans. Ford, GM, and Chrysler all pay engineers big bucks to create new designs and body styles for automobiles, so it's amazing just how few catch the eye of the American public. God, on the other hand, continues to crank out unique human being styles. Park yourself at an airport, mall, or busy street corner and see how different we (people) all are. Not only do we all have a different looking earth-suit, but we act, walk, think, believe, and talk differently as well.

Believe it or not, you will *not* always like or agree with people you come in contact with throughout your life. With that thought in mind (don't think too hard about it—it will give you a headache), realize you need to get along with those you don't see eye to eye with. Whether it is your parents, fellow employees, teammates, or associates, you need to get on their turf and learn that those strange folks could be a nice balance for you. They may be just what you need to sharpen and help mold your character. You won't see the benefit if you avoid or cut them down. Open your heart and learn from them, even as different and freakish as they may appear at first. Go ahead, step off your turf onto theirs and reap the benefit of seeing value in everyone. Go on...take the field.

Who bugs you the most to be around? Why? What gifts could they have? Why is it good to hang around an opposite of you? Get on someone else's turf, okay?

Mouth Trap

Tongue

"Keep your tongue from evil and your lips from speaking deceit." Psalms 34:13

"Sticks and stones may break my bones, but words will *never* hurt me." NOT! Who ever wrote that perverted poem must not be living in the same world I am. They (words) are one of the few things that can both build up and tear down. They consist of nouns, verbs, adverbs, prepositions, conjugations, pronouns, adjectives, compounds, prefixes, and suffixes. You can express, utter, promise, articulate, corrupt, inform, negotiate, and interject with them. The mouth is the starting line and the ear is the finishing line of our words. The tongue is a muscle, the strongest muscle in our body (due to intense workout), and our ears are wimpy (from lack of exercise). Why is it so easy to talk and so hard to listen?

Our government is constantly trying to fight the uphill battle of domestic violence in our society, yet one weapon we seem to overlook is the tongue...it's lethal. Very few times have I seen someone get praised or asked for an autograph for being a *good listener.* I love the saying "It's better to remain silent and be thought of as a fool, than to open your mouth and remove all doubt." Now, don't hear me wrong, there is a time to speak, but not *all* the time. Communication is a two way street...talking and listening. Go through a day listening more than talking and see what you learn. Don't trap yourself with your mouth (open mouth, insert foot). Believe you me, you'll stay out of a lot of trouble by keeping that dude shut more than open, and less people get hurt that way too.

Are you a good listener? When you're nervous, what do you do—talk or listen? Why do we learn more when we listen? What can you do today to make yourself a better listener?

The Beat Of A Different Drummer

Music

"Whatever is true, honorable, right, pure, lovely, of good repute, if there is any excellence and if anything worthy of praise, let your mind dwell on these things." Philippians 4:8

You hear it in restaurants, airports, cars, elevators, hospitals, dental clinics, and office lobbies. It might be ragtime, jazz, rock, polka, waltz, rumba, cha-cha (what?), soul, swing, country, pop, bolero, or blue grass. It's sound may be vocal, instrumental, lullaby, big band, symphonic, or easy listening. Tired of this yet? It's written with keys, bars, clef, signature, notes, slurs, pitches, chords, and flows from arrangements, compositions, melodies, performances, concerts, and orchestras. Come on, take a wild guess what's being described here. Hint: it starts with an *m*, ends with a *c,* and it ain't *microscopic*. It's music!

Music runs in and out of our ears and minds daily, depositing unscreened thoughts. It strikes me ironic that God created us with one mouth and two ears. One can be open and shut at will, the others stay open all the time, like an all-night truck stop. We must be cautious what we let into our minds through those two doors called ears. Why? Because what gets funneled through the ears may eventually end up etched on the stone tablets of the heart. Variety and taste is the name of the game when it comes to music selection. We all have different likes and dislikes, but one thing is true for all...music conveys a strong message. The problem is not the music itself, but the words that escort those tiny tunes. Guard your heart. Be picky about who and what you let preach to you through songs. Your mind (thoughts) will eventually dictate the feelings of your heart. If your heart (your livelihood) becomes hardened from false counsel then you're in deep trouble. Don't be deceived. Listen to the beat of a different drummer.

What kind of music do you listen to? Do you think Jesus would listen to it too? Why or why not? Why is Christian music a healthy alternative?

The Family Shrine

Television

"Your eyes will see strange things, and your mind will utter perverse things." Proverbs 23:33

Before you read this devotional I have a field trip I want you to take. You don't have to drive, in fact, all you need to do is walk a few feet. Take a stroll into your family room (that's the one with the TV in it) and take a look around. Okay, do you see the sofa, game table, E-Z Boy recliner, a few left-over papers, and the family shrine? What's the shrine? It's the TV set—the focal point of the family room. Americans have made it a tradition to put the television smack-dab in the middle of the action. It's like TV has become some sort of god in our homes. We should bronze those things and put them in a museum of technical history for future generations to gawk over.

It scares me to think how valuable we make a box of fuses, bulbs, and wires. We have cable, pay-per-view, satellite dishes, and video technology as our main source of communication, education, and malfunction. Whatever happened to family game nights, playing catch in the yard, going on evening walks, or just talking to one another? Why have we replaced family fun with the remote control? Television is one thing that can barge into our homes and say what it wants to say without being invited or even knocking before entering. Our minds are being filled with false philosophies and twisted theology and we sit and think, "It's not hurting me." Our lives are being molded by a foreign source, instead of God's scripture. See if there is any way you can re-arrange your furniture to make the TV as much of a centerpiece as a bathroom. Make it a household rule that if anyone or thing doesn't speak truth you set it in a corner. The TV will be the *first* to be punished for a foul mouth. The average person in America today spends fourteen and a half years watching the tube from age five to sixty-five. Don't waste one sixth of your life "vegging out." Make that move!

Where is the TV in your house? It is a shrine you glare at daily? What productive things could you be doing instead? Try a week without TV and see if your life isn't more productive and less ritualistic.

Rules

"Now the deeds of the flesh are evident, which are: immorality, impurity, sensuality, idolatry, sorcery, enmities, strife, jealousy, outburst of anger, disputes, dissentions, factions, envying, drunkenness, carousing, and things like these, of which I forewarn you just as I have forewarned you that those who practice such things shall not inherit the Kingdom of God." Galatians 5:19-21

Close your eyes for a moment and imagine a football game with no end zone, a basketball game with no hoop, a golf course with no fairway, a tennis match with no net, and a track or swim meet with no lanes. Now, correct me if I'm wrong, but that would be the ultimate in confusion. Basketball without sidelines, referees, or a goal is rugby. If you have ever been on a canoe or raft trip down a long river in Colorado you know the ride is defined by the beauty of cliffs that grow out of the river banks up to the clouds. Boundaries communicate a standard set by a scholar of the game and help produce a sport that's fun, yet fair to all.

Whether you like them or not, agree or disagree, you live in a civilization that has a few rules and boundaries. They are in place to help, not hurt you. Why a speed limit? So you don't kill yourself or others. Why gun laws? So no one shoots you. Why a judicial system? So everyone goes by the same laws. God has set in place rules and laws that are there for your benefit. The Ten Commandments are not a list of suggestions. Do yourself a favor and stay in the bounds that God laid down. It makes life so much easier and less painful. God is not some cosmic kill-joy looking to punish you for living. He desires to provide a wonderful, fulfilling, joyful game of life...just stay in bounds or you'll lose.

Why are there rules? Why do sports have boundaries—to help the game or destroy it? Do you play in or out of bounds in God's game most of the time? What can you do to stay in bounds more often? Accountability?

Cow Talk

Fellowship

"We who had sweet fellowship together." Psalms 55:14

There is nothing quite like driving down a country road where pastures are sewn together like a patchwork quilt and livestock bask in the sun, ignoring life's hectic pace. Have you ever pulled over on the side of the road and watched a pasture of cows grazing? Rolling down the window and letting a gust of wind fill your car with that fragrant aroma of cow poop is breath taking (no pun intended). If you treat yourself to this exciting event, you'll notice that cows seem to be in their own little world. They seem to be oblivious that they are surrounded by a fleet of fellow bovine.

This may not be profound to you, but it was to me. Pull your life over in a mall, airport, school, business, or church and see if homosapien (humans) patterns don't mirror that of the heifer. We have created a monster of fellowship and communication. We are so hi-tech in our telecommunications world, yet we are sub-cavemen in our capability to function as a team. We go about our busy agendas and rarely stop to talk, visit, or exchange thoughts with anyone (at times even our own family members). "Cow talk" has replaced communication in our culture. To survive we need to slow down, pull over, chill out, and visit with others...that's how we realize how unique everyone is. Cows don't need to talk, because their destiny lies between two buns at McDonald's. Your future is eternal and you need to get to know those going with you. Tell those who aren't in the right pasture where you're going and that they can go too...heaven, not a hamburger. Now, talk amongst yourselves!

Do you talk with others much or sit in a pasture and chew your own cud? Do you have fears of communicating to someone? Do you really talk to your family members? Why not? Why is communication so vital to your health.

To Be Called

God's Calling

"Who shall I send, and who will go for us? Then said I, Here I am, send me." Isaiah 6:8

You hear it from the pulpit at church to Christian social groups in conversation. Exactly what does it mean to be called? Do you feel you have a specific calling in life? How do you *really* know if you are called? These are all valid questions with simple answers. In this verse, God didn't address Isaiah specifically, Isaiah just overheard. Whether I hear God depends if my spiritual ears are turned on or not. "Many are called, but few are chosen," really means that some are not are listening. The chosen ones are those who walk so tight with God their radio dials are constantly tuned to His station. God didn't strong-arm Isaiah. Instead, Isaiah was in the presence of God, overheard the call, and realized the right response was, "Here I am, send me."

Forget the idea that God is gonna' storm into your life and lay a "calling" on you when He knows your response would be, "Let me think on it awhile." When Jesus chose His disciples there was an irresistible urging. They knew without question that if they didn't go, then God would find someone else who would. If we simply let the Holy Spirit dominate our thoughts, then the calling would be heard like a ship's horn, loud and clear, and so would the response, "Yes, Lord, I am here."

What is your calling? Has God called on you lately? Why or why not? Do you think your response would be like Isaiah's or the world's? Do you think that God knows your answer before you respond to Him? Write down when and what you may have been called to do, and what your response was.

Urged To Merge

Sex

"This is the will of God, your sanctification; that is that you abstain from sexual immorality." 1 Thessalonians 4:3

By the time a young person finishes high school, he will have spent eighteen thousand hours in front of the boob-tube (TV) and only twelve thousand hours in class. That is equal to more than two years spent staring at a hi-tech fish bowl. Daytime television contains fifty-percent more sexual references than "prime time," so you can see why it's so popular. Sixty percent of graduating teenagers say they learned about the "birds and bees" not from their parents, or sex education class, but via the television. Take a second and read through some facts that may just enlighten you about the urging from our society to have sex before marriage:

The average American teenager has had sex before their sixteenth birthday.

57% of high school and 79% of college students polled say they have lost their virginity.

80% of all teenage intercourse is spontaneous, not planned.

Reasons for having premarital sex are 1) peer pressure, 2) everyone's doing it, 3) curiosity, 4) gratification—not for love.

39% of high school and 58% of college students use contraceptives when having sex.

More people have died of AIDS than died in Vietnam.

(Statistics accumulated from USA Today, Journal of Marriage & Family, Center for Disease Control, Planned Parenthood)

Our sick society has discovered that exploiting young people for money is big business. We use sex to sell cigarettes, cars, toys, sports, and movies. You can't read, see, or hear anything today without catching a sexual reference. You, yes you, must decide where you stand and what you're standing for. Sex is not some sneaky, ugly, evil, ritualistic act portrayed by Hollywood, but a function designed specifically by God. What our Creator planned, the world has perverted. Resist the urge to merge and willfully wait until marriage...it is well worth it.

Why wait? Give reasons to wait. Why does God want us to wait until marriage? What steps can keep you out of a bad situation? Are you willing to wait?

Worship

"And he pitched his tent having Betel on the west and Ai on the east: there he built an altar." Genesis 12:8

The word *worship* means "to find worth" in something. Worship is giving God the best that He has given you—kind of a pay back mentality. Be cautious what you do with what you've been given. Whenever you are granted a blessing from above, make sure you give Him back that joy through your love and obedience. Just like manna when it was hoarded, so your blessings turn to rot when treated the same way. Bethel is the symbol of communion with God; Ai is the symbol of the world. Abraham, the father of the faithful, set up his tent between the two. The real measure of a mature Christian is how well he worships in the midst of total chaos. How often do you find time in your busy day to schedule a meeting with Him in private? There are three stages in our spiritual life—worship, waiting, and working. God's idea is that these three areas work together, not separately. They were always together in the life of our Savior as He found time for His Father, waited for His guidance, and worked to carry out His Father's will. This process will not just suddenly happen, it takes discipline and time. Find time today to commune with God to seek His will for your life today and what steps it may take to accomplish it.

What comes to your mind when you hear the word worship? Do you think you know how to worship God? What usually hinders your communion with God? Notch out thirty minutes today to worship God in the midst of a crazy Ai!

A Firm Foundation

Trials

"And everyone who hears these words of mine, and doesn't act on them, will be like a foolish man, who built his house on sand, and the rains came and so did the floods and the winds blew and burst against that house and it fell and great was its fall." Matthew 7:26-27

It's amazing what Realtors in our country will try to use as a selling point for a house. They parade around and point out all the features of a home, but seldom include the basement or structure of the foundation. Drive around any big city and you'll see gorgeous homes with beautiful yards, three car garages, hi-tech appliances, and all the bells and whistles. If the most awesome looking home in the country has a cracked foundation, it will be a heap of rubble in the long haul. Important questions the buyer needs to ask have nothing to do with colors, square footage, or floor plans. Pertinent questions need to deal first with the thickness of the foundation walls or slab, if re-bar was used, and what the foundation sits on (sand or base rock).

We as Christians build our foundation (lives) on one of these two substances...sand or rock. The strong rains of trials and gusty winds of uncertainty *will* come and if your life isn't firmly founded on God's truth (the rock), you *will* collapse. Church pews are filled, youth rallies are packed, families are functioning with folks who seem on the outside to have it "all together," yet when the tough times hit, they fall with a bang. Don't be one who builds his life on shifting sand that can't hold its ground through the thunderstorms of life. Trials will be a part of your life whether you're ready or not...here they come. Here is a little side note too...you can't lay a foundation (pour concrete) when it's raining—it's too late.

What is your foundation (life) built on? What will happen when the rains and wind beat you down? Will you fall or stand firm? How can you strengthen your foundation today? Get to work!

Goose Or Buffalo

Leadership

"Let him who is greatest among you become as the youngest, and the leader a servant." Luke 22:26

I heard some interesting stuff the other day concerning animals. Do you know the difference between a herd of buffalo and a flock of geese? Okay, besides the fact that one flies and one walks, one has feathers and one fur, one is on an old nickel and one honks like a horn. In the days of the old west, when Indians hunted buffalo for meat, they shot the lead buffalo of a stampeding herd and the rest would stop and freeze like statues at a museum. As for geese, when the lead goose flying in a "V" formation is shot, a replacement moves up from the flock and assumes the leader's position (taught you something didn't I...admit it). Now, it's interesting to me that in one case, leadership doesn't continue, but does in another. You tell me, which scenario appears to be the smartest of the two?

My definition of correct leadership tends to lean toward the style of the goose rather than the buffalo. Effective leadership is working your way out of the job by training, teaching, and placing others in positions to lead. The big, successful companies of today are run by a multitude of qualified, capable people who have been given specific functions in the company and fulfill those roles. No ministry, team, company, or organization should exist solely because of one person or it's future will be short-lived. If someone were to leave, or something were to happen to an organization you're a part of, is a person in place to keep it going or would it fold up like a wilted flower? Check it out, Jesus left and His twelve kept it going. Now, that's effective leadership!

Which team would you choose to be on...the buffalo or the geese? Why? Do you agree or disagree with this form of leadership?

Success

"Be careful to do all that is written in it (Bible) for then you will make your way prosperous and then you will have success." Joshua 1:8

Charles D. Tandy was born in 1918 and passed away at the young age of sixty in 1978. He was an energetic entrepreneur and risked it all as he acquired nine debt-ridden electronics stores. It took him a long and laboring fifteen years to turn the chain of nine into a mega-corporation of seven thousand stores which netted billions of dollars in 1963. Today this company still thrives on Mr. Tandy's energy. Shopping malls rarely exist without the familiar presence of Radio Shack. Texas Christian University (the college Tandy attended) named their business school building after him in memory of his dedication and success.

Father Abraham (you've sung the song before, haven't you?) was not always what you would call a genius. He fought against the odds all his life, yet was faithful to God every step of the way. He married Sarah who was barren (couldn't get pregnant) until by faith, she conceived a child at the unlikely age of ninety. After she gave birth to their son Isaac, God tested Abraham's faith again when He asked him to kill his only son on an alter. His faith won out yet again, and God showed Abraham grace and didn't require him to complete the test. We are asked by God each day to sacrifice all we are and have in order to claim success as ours. It takes maturity, strong belief, and a firm backbone. God will never ask you to do something you aren't capable of doing, but insists you trust and obey in order to be victorious in this Christian life. Abraham was named by God as the father of all generations...a title to be proud of.

If God asked you to sacrifice all you are and have for Him, would you? What do you have that stands in your way of achieving the success only God can grant you?

Privilege Not Program

Prayer

"Our Father who art in heaven hallowed be thy name." Matthew 6:9

I wrestled over the decision to include a devotional expounding on this bit of scripture. Why? Because Christians seem to have lost their grip on the purpose of prayer designated by God. I am not a "name it, claim it" Christian (don't tune me out...I'm not done). Yes, yes, yes, I do believe that our God is bigger than any sickness, any financial debt, or any situation we might get ourselves into, but I don't believe we can ask God for selfish things or ones that are incompatible with scripture and expect to receive them. Take a look at how Jesus taught His disciples to pray with the Lord's prayer. See if materialism rears its ugly head anywhere in this prayer. Instead, it teaches us to recognize God's position as God, praise His majesty, ask for daily survival tools, forgive us our mess-ups, and provide us strength to lessen our mistakes in the future.

My philosophy may appear to be that if I can't convince you, I'll confuse you, and I see by that look on your face, you're confused. Put it this way—prayer is a privilege, not a program. Prayer is an awesome moment when we enter into Jehovah's presence and communicate spiritually with Him face-to-face. Why do we let worldly thoughts enter our faith and convince us that the purpose for prayer is to gain acceptance or get our way? Don't forget that communication is not a one-way street when we talk and God listens. Part of an effective prayer life is that we "be still and know that I am God." Listen. You won't be able to hear Him in the midst of chaos. Find a Bethel (old testament place of worship) and be consistent in meeting your Savior there on a regular basis. Make your prayer life as practical as eating and breathing...it's a lot more fulfilling too! (No pun intended.)

How often do you pray? What gets in your way of having an effective daily prayer time? Do you see prayer as a privilege? How do you pray?

In The Rough

Trials

"Suffer hardship with me, as a good soldier of Christ Jesus." *2 Timothy 2:3*

I took up this sport at the tender age of ten, yet twenty-five years later I'm not much better. It's a goofy activity that uses lingo like "birdie, grain of grass, chip shot, lay-up, and in-the-rough." This game of madness is called golf. If you've tried your luck (I emphasize the word luck) at this sport, you know just how frustrating hitting a little white ball with a metal club toward a waving flag can be. In Texas we call it cow pasture pool—a more appropriate name for the way *I* play. You can watch the pros hack at it every Sunday afternoon on the PGA Tour at posh courses like Augusta, Sawgrass, and Pebble Beach. You can watch clubbers like me on public courses, trying their hand at hittin' it long and straight down the fairway. It takes me a little longer, but the object is to keep the ball out of the rough and on the nicely groomed fairways. Guess what though? Even the pros sometimes end up smackin' a few trees and landing in the rough, a long way from the hole.

Here is a lame yet profound thought—no matter how hard we try in our Christian lives, we will *all* end up in the "rough" sometimes. You tend to bear down more, concentrate, and often perform better when your ball lies in a tougher, rougher area. So it is in our lives, in rough times we tend to have deeper faith and bear down in our dependence on God. You see, the pros separate themselves from the amateurs, not by how well they perform on the easy fairways, but how they overcome rough shots. Make it a point in your life not to give up and head to the clubhouse of self-pity when you're in rough times, but bow up, dig in, and give it all you have. See if your life doesn't end up on the green, on track, ready for the next challenge. Catch this...you will (not optional) end up in the rough at times throughout your life because that's not only how you become a better golfer, but a faithful follower. Tee it up!

Where does your ball (life) lie right now? Fairway or rough? Where do you learn the most? How can you best get out of the rough and back in the fertile fairways of life?

Welcome Home

Heaven

"Our citizenship is in heaven." Philippians 3:20

In childhood's day, our thought of heaven,
Are pearly gates and streets of gold,
And all so very far away;
A place where portals may unfold,
Some far off distant day.
But in the gathering in the years,
When life is in the fading leaf,
With eyes perchance bedimmed with tears,
And hearts oft overwhelmed with grief,
We look beyond the pearly gates,
Beyond the clouds of grief's dark night,
And see a place where loved ones walk,
Where all is gladness and light.
And overall we see the face
Of Him who will bring us to our own,
Not too far off distant place,
For Heaven is, after all, just HOME!

Sue Milan

Just like the song says, "Heaven is a wonderful place, filled with glory and grace." Are you convinced there really is a distant destination of deity? How often does your mind drift away to dream of that refuge from pain? Can you imagine what this heaven is gonna' be like? Our residence is earth, but we all carry a foreign travel visa that states as a Christian, our citizenship is in heaven. Yes, the task on earth is difficult, so don't relax, opportunities are brief, so don't delay, the path is narrow, so don't wander, and the prize is glorious, so don't faint. Trust me, the ride is gonna' be far more impressive than anything Disney World has to offer. The place is gonna' be far more beautiful than St. Paul's Cathedral. The future is gonna' last far longer than life here on earth (vapor)...they call it eternity!

What do you think heaven will look like? Be like? Do you think of eternity on a time line or never ending? Do you think of your citizenship as being on earth or in heaven?

Gifts

"For the body is not one member but many." 1 Corinthians 12:14

A little boy was asked to write an essay on the different parts of the human body (anatomy). Here is what he wrote:

Your head is kind of round and hard, and your brains are in it and your hair too. Your face is the front of your head where you eat and make faces. Your neck is what keeps your head out of your collar and it's hard to keep clean. Your shoulders are sort of shelves where you hook your suspenders on. Your stummick is something that if you don't eat often enough it hurts, and spinach don't help none. Your spine is a long bone in your back that keeps you from folding up. Your back is always behind you no matter how quick you turn around. Your arms you got to have to pitch with and so you can reach the butter. Your fingers stick out of your hands so you can throw a curve and add up rithmetick. Your legs is what if you have not got two of, you can't get to first base. Your feet are what you run on, your toes are what get stubbed. And that's all their is of you, except what's inside, and I never saw that.

Just as the human earth-suit has many parts with specific functions, so do we as a Christian family. The problem seems to be that we function more as individuals than as a family. We seem to have inserted the letter "I" in the word team. We all are different in the way we look, talk, act, and function, but we have a common thread that is *supposed* to sew us together—Christ. Each one of us brings to the table a whole new set of goals and gifts used to further the kingdom as a body of believers. Think about it (I'll wait here!)...the hand has a separate function from the foot, the foot is different than the knee, the knee does not perform as an eye, and so on. As you look around, you'll notice that each Christian brings a different gift or talent to the family and together we mount a mighty force for the Kingdom. Now let's go team!

What do you feel your gifts are? Are you, at times, intimidated by others' gifts? Why? Do you function as a part or separate from the body?

Real Meaning Of Christmas

Christmas

"Where is He who has been born King of the Jews? For we saw His star in the east, and have come to worship Him." Matthew 2:2

Only in California would you find this. San Jose's city fathers ordered the traditional crèche (nativity scene) removed from the annual Christmas display in the park, citing, "sensitivity to the city's non-Christian population." Just a few weeks before this decision though, they approved spending five hundred thousand dollars for a huge concrete statue honoring Quetzalcoatl—the ancient Aztec snake god. Now, help me out here...is that art? Anyway, the city elders finally woke up and clued in, partly due to two hundred thousand protesters who flooded city hall, and allowed the nativity to be re-instated temporarily, but the snake god is there to stay...a tribute to mankind's afflicted ways of handling conflict, and a triumph of multi-culturalism. Interestingly enough, the federal district court ruled that the snake god was permissible because nobody worships it anymore. A figure of the baby Jesus in the nativity scene was removed because He is still worshipped.

It happened two thousand years ago, continues today, and will forgo tomorrow, when folks try to rid Jesus from the meaning of Christmas. We do it today when our holiday traditions consist only of gift buying, opening, and exchanging. Remove Jesus from the nativity scene and you have a gathering of big-wigs in a stable starring at an empty feed trough, without hope. Jesus brings to the scene joy, hope, and a future that's better than the present. Next time you celebrate Christmas, have a total blast tearing into the presents, hanging lights, decorating the tree, singing carols, visiting with relatives, and stuffing your face, but don't forget the "reason for the season." I'll give you a clue...it ain't an Aztec snake god!

What does Christmas mean to you? What do you look forward to during this festive season? Is Jesus a part of your traditions? What can you do to make Him a centerpiece in your nativity (life)?

A KNOCK-OUT!

Sharing Christ

"When the kindness of God our Savior and His love for mankind appeared, he saved us, not because of righteous things we had done, but because of his mercy." Titus 3:4-5

It was one of those days when the fast lane got even faster. I drove up and parked in the lot of T.J. Rusk Inner-City Middle School in Dallas, Texas, waiting on my mom, who teaches there. Obviously, school had just ended because the yellow limos (school buses) were parading past to deliver kids to their homes. I was pondering what life in middle school was like when I noticed two boys about thirteen years old just being boys, kinda' mock (slap) fighting. You know what I'm talking about...releasing that excess educational energy that builds up throughout a day sitting behind a desk. It seemed to be two friends sparring until the jabs became punches, and the punches became down-right slugs, and I realized (I'm slow) I had a brawl on my hands. I jumped out of the car and ran to stop this main event. No one else seemed to care, but I for one, was not gonna' be an idle spectator to this foolishness. After a few close calls from stray punches, I settled the two boys down and began to sort through this madness.

After the blank stares, swollen knuckles, and winded breathing calmed, we got down to the source of the swings—nothing! That's right ladies and gentlemen, absolutely no reason for the fight except a big, fat..."because." They were best friends, neighbors, and get this—relatives. Why? (Let me ask one more time.) Why? What is happening to our world? This incident, in a few years, could end up in a stabbing or shooting. I'll tell you my thinking...we are a society on the edge of insanity, missing the key ingredient of Godly love—love for your neighbor, brother, sister, parents, friends. We as Christians have no choice but to show (notice I didn't say tell) this fallen world about Christ's love. Just continue to keep this little secret to ourselves (believers) and see how insane this planet will become...unbearable. Jump into the ring, throw a few love punches yourself and knock 'em out in an early round for Jesus...ding! ding!

How do you tell others of Jesus' love? Do you at all? Why or why not? How can you train yourself to do this? Will you?

The Bell Curve

Jesus

"Let us keep living by the same standard to which we have attained." Philippians 3:16

The bell curve has been as much a part of the American education system as recess and sack lunches. Teachers use this curve as a scale for fairness in the grading system. It was adopted by (Alexander Graham Bell...NOT!) our school systems to allow pupils to be graded with fairness and equality. The curve is a measuring tool for the teacher to judge whether a test was too difficult (or easy) and prohibits the entire class from receiving a failing grade. For instance, if one out of twenty-five students scores 100% then the teacher has a problem setting the curve. The teacher has to make a decision whether to fail the low scores and allow the one student to pass or question the superior student.

Jesus' classroom was the corrupt world in which He traveled. The test was righteousness verses worldliness. The consequence was death. You see, the high score only makes the low scores look even worse and messes up the grading system. I'd say that Christ did a good job of messing up the world standards of good and evil. He made the Pharisees seem not quite as good as they appeared to be on paper. He brought to light a new definition of real love. He broke the mold. The test results? Failure of a superior Savior by the world teachers, put to death as a thief, but exaltation to the throne of God the Father. Make straight A's in God's classroom and guess what...it's okay to flunk this world's tests. God's class is one you can't take again in the next semester (life)...so be on the "honor role."

Do you set the example at home, school, team, or with your peers? Why is it so important to be an *example* not a *follower* of this world?

Laughter

"A time to weep and a time to laugh." Ecclesiastes 3:4

We all need to grab a break from this treadmill of life from time to time. Since we are such creatures of habit (hence, sheep) we need to break the mold, spread our wings, and just be strange for a minute...totally out of character. The following list is an example of some strange things we can do to handle those tough times in life. You can add to this list or take away, but hopefully it will get your creative juices flowing down the funnel of fun. Take a look:

Pop some popcorn without putting the lid on.
Use your Mastercard to pay your Visa (just kidding).
When someone says, "Have a nice day," tell them you have other plans.
Forget the diet center and send yourself a candy gram.
Make a list of things to do that you've already done.
Dance in front of your pets.
Draw underwear on the natives in National Geographic.
Drive to work in reverse (a joke).
Reflect on your favorite episode of "The Flintstones" during class.
Refresh yourself: put your tongue on a frozen steel guardrail.
Start a funny rumor and see if you recognize it when it comes back.
Write a short story using alphabet soup.
Stare at people through a fork and pretend they are all in jail.
Make up a language and ask people for directions.
Put your clothes on backwards and pretend nothing's wrong (walk backward).

Note: these ideas are *not* to be taken literally; they're just thought provokers. You make up your own list. Live a little!

How often do you laugh? How do you handle stress? Do you take yourself too seriously at times? Why?

Sex

"This is the will of God, your sanctification; that you abstain from sexual immorality." 1 Thessalonians 4:3

Talk about one heck of a mess we've gotten ourselves into now. America has by far the highest reported rate of AIDS infected people in the industrial world, and the number of cases diagnosed continues to multiply as we speak (or read). A total of 361,164 cases were reported through 1994. Nearly two-thirds of those have died. It's estimated that approximately one million Americans are infected with AIDS, that's one out of every 250 folks. According to a *USA Today* report, by the year 2000 it is predicted that everyone will know someone *personally* who has contracted and died from this killer virus.

The "politically correct" teaching that AIDS doesn't target any particular lifestyle continues to be popular. Now for the truth...if AIDS had not targeted a specific political activist group, it would probably have been brought under control long ago as other epidemics have been controlled by isolation and quarantines. It is too late to start now, or even consider, as the disease is spreading like a grass plains wild fire in summer, into the general population of America. Raising children in the midst of this epidemic is downright frightening. In most cases AIDS is a consequence for an immoral, impure lifestyle which seems to continue the thinking, "If it feels good, do it." We are to pray and have *sincere* compassion for individuals who are sick with this virus. Love the sinner, but learn how to hate (despise) the sin (immorality). Whether you think so or not...this is *your* problem now. God has ground rules for sex, not because He is some modern day kill-joy. It's because He cares! Morality in this country is better caught than taught. We need to focus in on the root of the issue, not just deal with the leaves.

What is morality? What do you see as immoral in our society? Does it effect you directly or indirectly? What can you do about it?

NOT ME!

Obedience

"Before I formed you in the womb I knew you, before you were born I set you apart; I appointed you as a prophet to the nations." Jeremiah 1:5

I've always admired the prophet Jeremiah and his willingness to be used as a tool in the Master's hand, a prophet to Judah. When God called him to his occupation in life, he was more than happy to fill the orders as a soldier in God's army. Like so many God calls to serve, Jeremiah immediately began making excuses why he *didn't* qualify. A prophet has to speak, so Jeremiah explained, "I don't know how to speak and I'm only a mere child (verse 16)." God patiently (as always) assured Jeremiah that he didn't need to be fearful of this position or any other. God communicates, "I will be with you and rescue you." I'm sure the word *rescue* raised some suspicion in Jeremiah as to what he was in for. Then an interesting thing happened—God touched Jeremiah's mouth and put His words there.

Why is it that God, with all of His might, continues to put up with us? We doubt, dodge, deliberate, defy, and deny Him, yet He still has the patience to "hang with us" through it all. You, as Jeremiah, were created for a specific purpose and have a reason for being here. The problem comes when we doubt the deity of His selection process. No one knows for what purpose or achievement you were created, but you *are* capable because He qualified you with honors. Don't doubt God's intent or plan, just obey it. Don't question His judgment, just submit to it. Don't hide from His calling, just do it...sound like a catchy shoe slogan?

Why were you born? For what purpose do you see yourself existing? Are you listening to God's direction? Why or why not?

Discipleship

"Go therefore and make disciples of all nations, baptizing them in the name of the Father, Son and the Holy Spirit." Matthew 28:19

If you've been so fortunate to have taken this class, you're educated, and if not, you will be. It teaches you about "the birds and bees," you know...those special features males and females have in order to reproduce another person. You blush, squirm, duck your head, bug your eyes, and feel more than a bit uncomfortable, but you learn. You learn the miracle of life that takes place when a female and male have a physical relationship and *presto,* a bambino. It is amazing how the child grows up and genetically and habitually take on the appearance and mannerisms of their parents...a "clone," you might say.

As Christians we are told (not asked) to reproduce (spiritually, not physically) our own type—that type looks like Christ, not us—and make disciples. First, you must be a follower before you can reproduce, an important process we must continue or our species will become extinct. Here are seven things that it takes to reproduce a disciple:

Able to walk your talk (model it).
Able to teach the basic *truths of the Bible.*
Able to communicate basic skills of life.
Able to teach basic ministry skills.
Able to confront in love when needed.
Able to impart the vision to your disciple to go and disciple someone else (reproduce).
Able to stick with it despite disappointment and slow learning.

You see, the authority on electricity is *not* an electrician, but an eel. Why? Because an electrician studies and learns about electricity, but never touches it. An eel is made of it, so it's his source of being. As Christians, we need to not only study about Christ, but allow Him to become the source of energy that enables us to function every day. Find someone to disciple (pour your life into) so that they in turn can do the same for another to reproduce our type in a lost world.

Are you a disciple? Explain. Are you teaching discipleship to someone else? Why not? Who can you disciple?

Worldliness

"For all that is in the world, the lust of the flesh and the lust of the eyes and the boastful pride of life, is not from the Father, but is from the world." 1 John 2:16

The more you look like Christ, the more the world is gonna' treat you like Him. It is a frightening thing when you arrive at the point in your spiritual journey that you decide to truly be an ambassador for Jesus. The scary part about it is that when you pledge allegiance to the flag of America, you live and associate as a citizen of America. However, when you pledge allegiance to Christ, you disassociate yourself from the world and proclaim heaven as your homeland. Being a Christian is more than walking down the aisle, attending church, or wearing a cross. The price Jesus paid was a heavy one. You may not get ridiculed and alienated when you associate with a church, youth group, Bible study, or religious movement, but you *do* when you say, "I'm a follower of Jesus Christ." The penalty (really a privilege) is when you finally come to that point of locking arms with Christ.

Years ago a country song summed up what being a real Christian in a real hurting world is all about..."If you don't stand for something, then you'll fall for anything." The "something" has *got* to be Jesus. The "anything" might be sex, money, status, cults, and so on. Ask God to plant deep in the chambers of your heart a soul of *passion* to follow Him, knowing that the cost will include pain and suffering. I don't know where folks get off on all this hoop-la that Christianity is a total joy ride. Either I am reading a different Bible or they are not hearing the truth that the adventure, called Christianity, takes endurance and perseverance. Pain is a part of the curriculum of God's classroom, so prepare for a tough test, but one worth passing.

Why is association with Christ so costly? To whom do people say you are pledged? How can you handcuff yourself to Christ from now on? Why is ridicule a part of Christianity?

BUD BUSTER

Spiritual Growth

"And he will be like a tree firmly planted by streams of water, which yields its fruit in its season and its leaf does not wither and whatever he does, he prospers." Psalms 1:3

Don't get the idea that I'm some kind of botanist (dude who studies plants). In fact, I made a whopping "D" in that class in college. I would like to share with you though, and I promise not to bore you like my college professor did me, a little mind tickler on plant growth. Let's say that Joe Citrus Farmer wants to increase the productivity of certain fruit bearing plants, so he does just the opposite of what you'd expect. During the season the plant begins to bud, Joe C. cuts off each and every bud (the bud is the area of the plant that produces fruit) from every limb. Now, as brainless as that may sound, it allows the plant to take all the energy and nutrients needed to produce good fruit, and send them to the root system to strengthen and provide growth to that vital area. We all know that for any tree, plant, or shrub, the most important area is the root system (kinda' like the heart of a human body).

Now watch me pull a rabbit out of the hat and try to tie this example into a life-practical analogy. Visualize God, our Father, as the farmer on a large fruit-producing plantation, with you and me as the citrus crop. He has to do some bud snipping in order for us (His children) to become fruit bearers to this unfruitful world. Yes, the snipping process hurts like heck, but it's all for a specific purpose. Our foundation (roots) will be deepened and strengthened to survive the long, hard, cold winter months (our life on earth), so that in our time to produce, the crop will be plentiful. Get it? God wants us to show off our juicy fruit to a world of sour grapes. Snip, snip!

Why is it so important for us to produce healthy fruit for God? What slows your growth down? What is fruit used for today? Are you producing fat or anemic fruit? Are you willing to be snipped so you can grow deeper roots?

Maturity

"Speaking the truth in love, we are to grow up in all aspects into Him, who is the head, even Christ." Ephesians 4:15

In his book, *First Things First*, author Roger Merrill tells of a business consultant who decided to landscape the grounds around his home. He hired an extremely knowledgeable woman with a doctorate in horticulture. Because he was very busy and traveled a lot, the business consultant emphasized again and again the need to create a garden that would require little or no maintenance on his part. He insisted on automatic sprinklers and other labor-saving devices. Finally, the horticulturist stopped him and said, "There's one thing you need to deal with before you go any further. If there's no gardener, there's no garden!"

Gang, there are *no* labor-saving devices for growing a garden of spiritual virtue. Becoming a person who produces spiritual fruit requires time, attention, and daily care. I am amazed at the number of long-standing Christians still nursing on the spiritual bottle, instead of maturing on spiritual meat. This immaturity is directly related to the lack of time invested in growth habits such as daily time in scripture study, prayer, and learning to share faith through discipleship or evangelism. Great athletes don't just wake up one day as superstars...it takes years of consistent practice. The old saying that "practice makes perfect" is incomplete...*perfect* practice makes perfect. Practice for spiritual growth in the game of life just as diligently as you would for an athletic or scholastic competition. You *will not* become mature until you see the value and importance of consistent practice and nurturing of your faith. Tend to *your* garden of faith every day, planting, weeding, watering, and harvesting. Otherwise don't be puzzled when you look up in a few years to see a withered, wilted, worthless harvest of spiritual fruit in your life.

How mature are you in your relationship with Christ? Do you tend to your spiritual garden daily or do you lean toward labor-saving devices to do it for you? What steps can you take to cultivate your maturity? List them out as goals and give them to a friend to hold you accountable.

Stubbornness

"But these people are stubborn and have a rebellious heart." Jeremiah 5:23

Between two farms near Valleyview, Alberta, you will find two fences running parallel for half a mile, only two feet apart. Why two fences when only one is necessary? Two farmers named Paul and Oscar had a disagreement that erupted into an all out feud. Paul wanted to build a fence between their land and split the cost, but Oscar disagreed and refused to contribute. Paul wanted to keep cattle on his land, so he went ahead and built the fence on his own. Afterward, Oscar said to Paul, "I see *we* have a fence now." "What do you mean *we*?" Paul replied. "I had the property line surveyed and built the fence two feet inside my property line, which means some of my land is outside the fence. Now if any of your cows step foot on my property, I'll shoot 'em for trespassing." Oscar knew this was not a joke, so when he eventually decided to use the land adjoining Paul's pasture, he was forced to build a second fence only two feet from the first. Oscar and Paul are both gone now, but their double fence stands as a monument to the high price paid for stubbornness.

It's amazing just what sparks a "tiff" between people. Often folks are all out to win, with no regard for the feelings or concerns of others. It's the "my way or the highway" mentality that gets most of us in trouble. Why can't we have a servant's attitude and heart when it comes to dealing with each other? Don't you realize we were all placed on the same planet for a reason? "Getting along" is only difficult when we create an environment (with attitude and behavior) that makes it difficult. What if Christ had an attitude that only exalted Me, Myself, and I? (Answer: We'd be in a pickle about now!) Learn to live in harmony, not harassment. Give a little and you'll get a lot.

Are you a stubborn person? What makes you want to be stubborn (specific areas)? Does having a "my way" attitude make life easier or more difficult? How can you work on that area?

DIE HARD

Commitment

"But thanks be to God that, though you used to be slaves to sin, you wholeheartedly obeyed the form of teaching to which you were entrusted." Romans 6:17

In a small, hole-in-the-wall doughnut shop in Grand Saline, Texas one cool, damp morning a young couple was sitting in the booth next to the cashier. Judging by his attire of Red Wing boots and Carhart over-alls, the young man might have been in farming, and she was wearing a gingham dress. After finishing the glazed doughnuts, he got up to pay the bill, while she was noticed not getting up to follow him. He soon returned and stood in front of her as if reporting for duty. She reached up to put her arms around his neck as he lifted her from the booth, revealing her full-body brace. As he proudly (not shamefully) carried her through the double doors and situated her comfortably in the pick-up truck, everyone in the shop watched, mouths wide open. No one said a word until a waitress remarked, almost reverently, "He took his vows seriously."

Jumpin' Jack Flash! Now, if that story doesn't well up your tear ducts I don't know what will. You seldom see folks *that* committed to anything anymore. Our world breeds a species trained to bail out when the heat is turned up. There are so few committed to their jobs, faith, marriages, friendships, causes, or daily disciplines. Why? Have we forgotten the meaning of commitment? To be committed is to be like a car battery that can "withstand the extremes" and still serve its purpose. Life is just not fair, and tough times will be waiting for you no matter where you live or how far you run. Inject a "stick-to-it" attitude in your life now, at a young age. You will always play in the game of life like you practice when no one is looking. Make a decision (commitment) and don't waver from it no matter how tough it gets...good thing Jesus did!

Are you considered by others as being a committed person? Why or why not? What could help you to become more committed in your faith, family, friends, etc. In the future? Do it!

ARMCHAIR QUARTERBACKS

Counsel

"As you judge others, so you will yourselves be judged." Matthew 7:1

They always know the way to go...and never go themselves.
It is easy to make decisions...when the responsibility is not yours!
It's easy to know what to do...when you don't have to do it!
They always know what to do...and never have to do it.

Some of the most peculiar creatures that roam our streets are those who are free from responsibility, yet tell those responsible what to do. The slang for these aggravating, vocal critics who always seem to have the answer is "armchair quarterbacks." There is a huge chasm between the spectator in the bleachers and the participant on the field. Now, don't limit your thinking to the sphere of sports...let's use everyday life. There are experts who pontificate on every conceivable issue in life. These armchair quarterbacks never seem to make any mistakes. This doesn't mean that advice and opinions are wrong...that's what democracy is made of. The problem lies in the spirit (motivation) of the critic.

This spirit should always be sensitive to the burden of decision(s) borne by the one being criticized. Always place yourself in the other's shoes before you "give them a piece of your mind." More often than not, the critic doesn't know all there is to know about a certain situation or the decision making process. Armchair play-calling doesn't hold water when the consequences don't ultimately rely on self. So, if you're one of those folks who always tend to call the plays (answers) from the sidelines, then take a chill pill. Extend grace and understanding to those who are on the front-lines of the decision making process.

Do you see yourself as a critic or an encourager? Why? Do you like to point the finger at poor play-calling? Why?

The Boa Constrictor

Satan

"Now the serpent was more crafty than any beast of the field which the Lord God had made." Genesis 3:1

I have a *big* problem with reptiles that slither on their bellies and scare the pants off people. In college my bright roommate decided life wasn't exciting enough, so he purchased a rather large boa constrictor snake. That's right...a third roomie—one that eats people and never sleeps. My roommate (not the slimy one) fed his new found companion (named Bert) rats for an afternoon snack. Yuck-eee! You talk about gross! Can you believe you can actually purchase rats to use for snake food? Don't rats have a humane society to protect them? (Guess not...who has a rat for a pet anyway? Don't answer that!) Let me get to my point, I always thought that constrictors squeezed their prey to death, then ate it whole. Not true—these snakes wrap their slithery bodies around a victim, wait for them to exhale, and squeeze down. Wait for an exhale, squeeze down, another exhale, squeeze tighter until the prey can't inhale again and finally dies.

Do you recall anyone in the Bible who could possibly go by the code name "Serpent?" I believe he first made his debut on stage in the Broadway hit, "In The Garden." Satan *is* (notice I didn't say *was*) a constrictor of life who squeezes the joy out of life when we fall prey to sin. Whether pre-marital sex, compulsive dishonesty, bitterness, or hatred, sin will choke you out like a candle with no oxygen. Steer clear of the serpent and his deceiving tactics of tightening that will result in death (physical and spiritual). Believe you me, having a snake as a roommate was bad, but as a master, it would be worse.

Why was Satan called a serpent? What does it mean in the verse above that the snake was more crafty than any beast of the field? What does Satan tighten down on in your life to squeeze the joy out of being a Christian?

Betrayed

Betrayal

"The Son of Man is to go, just as it is written of Him; but woe to that man by whom the Son of Man is betrayed! It would have been good for that man if he had not been born." Matthew 26:24

Talk about a subject that can bring your blood to a rapid boil. There is not one poor soul who reads this that has not been betrayed in some form or fashion (guess what...more to come). Jesus had a front row seat when it came to betrayal. Judas, the betrayer, was not only trusted and respected in his community of converts, but was a dog-gone disciple. Better yet, Judas sold out for a measly fifty-two bucks (thirty pieces of silver), betraying his so-called mentor, Jesus. How do you handle it when you are betrayed by a good friend? What is your first reaction? Is it Christ-like?

It is still true today that people sell their souls for the love of money. Money can make a woman a whore and a man a pimp. It can turn a shepherd into a skunk, make business go belly-up (broke), and turn an athlete into a liability. Now that we have identified the problem, what is the solution when you've been dealt a bad hand from a friend? What I'm about to say goes totally against the norm, and only you and God could pull it off. Ready? (Is the anticipation killing you?) Do two things when you have been betrayed. These are not secrets, Jesus did them with Judas. First, pray for their (the person's who betrayed you) conviction of the wrong doing. (Note: don't pray for their punishment...that's the world's way.) Second, pray for their forgiveness through *you*...the victim. (Note: extend grace to them, not judgment.)

Okay, has it sunk in enough for the steam to rise from the top of your head? These two simple steps will clear you of any bitterness and anger that ultimately will eat at you like cancer. Plus, it will be an example of what real Christ-like living is all about.

Have you ever been betrayed by a friend? How did you react? Was it like Jesus did offering Judas the first morsel of food as the honored guest?

Attitude

"Have this attitude in yourself which is also in Christ Jesus." Philippians 2:5

They say there are two types of people in our world—those who *read* stories, and those who *make* stories. I happen to have the temperament of the latter, in case you haven't noticed. Well, one of my new found hobbies is riding a Harley-Davidson "soft-tail" motorcycle around the beautiful Colorado Rocky Mountains on a warm, sunny day. There is nothing quite like rounding up a bunch of riding buddies, dropping any agenda, and heading for the mountains. I think one of the reasons I enjoy this new adventure is that when I'm on the back of a Harley Hog, I've got an *attitude.* That's right, you have never seen the likes of "too cool for school" looks I can give passing motorists when I'm ridin' with the pack.

You hear about folks with attitudes a lot these days. Just what does it mean? Where does an attitude take you? An attitude is a position, stand, belief, or state of mind. Get this one—we as Christians are to have an attitude. Frankly, this attitude should be quite different from the worldly attitude seen more often, since it is a Christ-like one. An attitude will give you altitude if it's the right kind, and dig you a grave if it's the wrong kind. An attitude reflects *who you are* and *what you believe.* Ask yourself what kind of attitude you suggest to the folks you come in contact with. What influences your attitudes? Is it emotion or false feelings? Is it your environment? Do you act differently according to who you are with or are you consistent in your actions?

Get an attitude! (The Christ-like type.)

First Impressions

Friendship

"Greet one another with a holy kiss of love." 1 Peter 5:14

There used to be a TV commercial where the punch line was, "You never get a second chance for a first impression." Oooh, how important that sentiment is when it comes to developing quality relationships. A good first impression can either take you a long way or put you in the ditch. Christians, without a doubt, should be the forerunners when it comes to making a good first impression on people. There has to be a balance between doing what is needed and over-doing it. Ask yourself this question...what do people say about you after you meet them for the first time? Do they feel encouraged and energized, or do you leave them tired?

I have a few basic suggestions that I hope you will try out (if you're not doing them already) when you first meet someone. Here they are in "Cliff Note" form:

Look them in the eye.
After hearing their name, say it five times to yourself.
Stand tall and be excited about their acquaintance.
Ask questions about them.
Show interest in their answers by responding with phrases like, "That's great!," "How exciting!," or "That's neat to know!"
Don't become distracted or lose eye contact during a conversation.
End the conversation by saying their name and, "It has been a pleasure talking with you."
Always use Mr., Mrs., or Miss if the person is older than you (until they tell you to do otherwise).
Always be respectful, polite, and courteous.

I hope that you can use these tools to make a good first impression. Remember *you* are the salt and light to a dark world and good impressions definitely season a relationship and light the way for friendship.

Practice the above steps when you next meet someone for the first time. Practice with your parents or a friend.

Casting

Prayer

"Casting all your anxiety upon Him, because He cares for you." 1 Peter 5:7

There is nothing quite like being the father of three boys and taking them on a little father-sons fishing outing. We went to a private area (not open to general public) called Dogwood Canyon, located in the Ozark Mountains of Missouri. I'd heard the spring fed stream was loaded with trophy size rainbow and brown trout, and they weren't kidding! I named the first fish my oldest boy caught Moby Dick. Get the picture? We had the time of our lives casting our lures into the stream and on every cast, within a matter of seconds, catching Jaws II on our hooks. Even though we did the "catch and release" thing, we made a memory on the trip of a lifetime.

I learned a spiritual lesson that day about casting and catching. I learned how much fun the art of casting is and what rewards come from such an elementary effort. God calls us to cast our hooks of life (anxiety in tough times) into the calm waters of our Creator and catch that peace that surpasses all understanding. God wants your problems because He knows you can't control them and He can. God is on the diet of eating problems for breakfast and you starve Him by not letting Him eat yours. To cast, means to take your bag full of stress to the foot of the cross through prayer, lay them down, and walk away. That's right...walk away and don't look back. Casting your cares will free you up to...who knows...maybe go fishin'?

How do you handle your problems? Who fixes your life for you? How often do you cast your cares on Him because He cares for you?

Coach Bumble-Bee

Commitment

"You became obedient from the heart to that form of teaching to which you were committed." Romans 6:17

He was like no man I'd ever seen or been around in all my years. If you looked up the word self-discipline in the dictionary, you'd find his picture next to it. He was a boxing coach for a youth club out of Seattle, Washington, and was training two teenage boxers for a national match that could lead to the 1996 Olympics. The tournament was scheduled to take place in Colorado Springs at the Olympic Training Facility where three hundred and fifty young boxers were trying to be the next Foreman, Frazier, or Ali. This coach went by the name "Coach Bumble-Bee," because aeronautically, bumble-bees shouldn't be able to fly since their wings are too small for the size of their bodies. But the bees don't know that, so they fly anyway.

Coach Bumble-Bee, now fifty years old, was the driver in a serious bus accident that left him paralyzed from the waist down. For five and a half years he managed his life from a wheelchair until one day, after years of prayer and exercise, Coach began moving his legs again. Today, Coach Bumble-Bee is walking, running, lifting weights, and jumping rope with his team members as he works out *daily* with them in vigorous training.

What faith! What determination! What discipline! What a deal! Told he would *never* walk again by physicians, but today not only walking, but running. I learned just through watching him work out with his boxers what it means to "never give up on God." The key ingredient to faith is *commitment.* Trust in God that He is bigger than theories, doctors' analysis, and scientific data. You can be a bumble-bee too if you will turn a deaf ear to the crowd of doubters and focus on the Savior. God is and always will be bigger than any problem or situation you get yourself into. If you don't believe me...just go watch the bumble-bee fly.

What does it mean to you to never give up? What makes you want to give up in tough times? What could you do to deepen that never-say-die attitude? Who could help you? Call 'em.

Money

"The root of all kinds of evil is the love of money." 1 Timothy 6:10

All right, let's test our trivia knowledge. You only have thirty minutes to complete this test. Please use a number two pencil and remember...no cheating or wandering eyes. Begin now:

Questions concerning American money:

What is a torn bill worth?

Who is the only women to be on a bill? When?

Who's picture is on the $1, $2, $5, $10, $20, and $50 bill?

How long is a bill used before it is recalled by the US Treasury for wear and tear?

What do the words "E Pluribus Unum" mean? What language is that?

Whose job is it to find counterfeiters?

In what cities are coins minted?

On what kind of paper are bills printed?

Okay, pencils down. How do you think you did? This devo relates to us all, because we all deal with its subject daily. Street names are cabbage, cash, green, jack, chips, bucks, change, two-bits, moolah, lucre, gelt, mazuma, red cents, or boodle. No matter what you call it, it's the good old dollar. You can't live with it and you can't live without it. It buys, separates, orchestrates, and devastates. It changes from one pocket to the next every second of our lives. Money though, is not the problem...the *love* of money is. It can make you happy as a lark one minute and send you into depression the next. Gang, money, if handled wrong or idolized, will destroy your life. Money is useful and can be a good thing if you don't fall in love with it. Steer clear of this monster of humanity or your life will end in one heck of a wreck. You'll always find those who have just as much chance roping the wind as finding fulfillment and satisfaction in money.

Answers:

3/5 or more = full amount; 3/5 or less = 1/2 value

Martha Washington in 1886

$1-Washington; $2-Jefferson; $5-Lincoln; $10-Hamilton; $20-Jackson; $50-Grant

18 months

"One from many" in Latin

Secret Service (and you thought they only guarded the President)

Denver; Philadelphia; San Francisco; West Point (gold only)

Paper with no pulp (regular paper has pulp in it)

How do you handle your money? Do you hoard it? Do you share it with others? Who ultimately owns all money?

Fashion

"Glorify God in your body." 1 Corinthians 6:20

A trend is defined as a social movement or surge in a specific area in our culture. Noticed recently is the adornment trend of tattoos and piercing. It doesn't take an investigative journalist or a fashion consultant to see just how (no pun intended) ingrained these fashion statements have become. Crossing mono-sexual boundaries, these trends are now unisex. Tattoos show up on ankles, arms, hands, and places too risky to discuss. Piercing takes place not only in the ears, but the naval, nose, and lips. Such adornments are not a new idea to civilization, but the recoil of these trends is strong. It boils down to how followers of Christ keep the balance? When is it proper to follow a trend?

Now, I realize that this is a controversial issue. I think that Scripture gives us the parameters to decide how Christians are to conduct themselves. The question one needs to ask is why? Why do I feel the need to partake in the trend? The answer may lie in individual insecurities, rebellion, or expression of a particular image. On the other hand, the motive may be pure and undefiled. You need to do some soul searching and motive meddling to find the personal inner-answer for yourself. Ask yourself, no matter what the trend of the year is:

Why am I participating? (Motive)

What does scripture say about it? (Means)

What would Jesus do? (Mentor)

Who am I honoring? (Method)

Now, rely on the Holy Spirit and your conscience to direct your decision in the matter. Oh yeah, you probably noticed that I didn't really answer the question. You're right, Sherlock...that's because the decision is yours...I've already made mine.

So how do you feel about these two issues? Are you participating in either of them now? Why or why not?

God's Word

"Do not be deceived, God is not mocked; for whatever a man sows, this he will reap also." Galatians 6:7

USA Today, Time, Newsweek, Wall Street, Sports Illustrated, Washington Post, Reader's Digest, TV Guide, or People—they all deliver a message. Most of the time the message is delivered in a package of pain, distress, sorrow, devastation, and anguish (that's stuff I read and weep over). The old agricultural cliché, "you reap what you sow," is seen at every newsstand and on every magazine page. Our modern culture seems to reap a harvest better left tilled under in hopes of a more productive harvest the next year. Why do we sow the wrong seeds and expect the right crop? The crops of corruption should instead be the cultivation of Christ.

It seems as if this world has thrown out the seeds of a Savior and replaced them with the weeds of worldliness. God's untainted, undefiled, uncompromising written words of wisdom will produce a bountiful harvest if we only read it and reap it. To reap means to bring forth something. To sow means to invest in something. Our investment on a daily basis in God's word will reap a harvest of hope, happiness, and heaven. The key to a banner year with a rich harvest is *consistent* time spent in the Bible each day, whether it's an hour or ten minutes. They say it takes twenty-one days to develop a habit. Make scripture study a habit and you're guaranteed a bountiful harvest. Read it and reap!

What gets in your way of spending fifteen to twenty minutes in The Word each day? What time of day can you set aside? Who can you get to hold you accountable each day?

Virtual Reality

Person of Christ

"Reality, however, is found in Christ." Colossians 2:17

I was on my way to Virginia, flying from Denver to Atlanta, when boredom hit and I succumbed to thumbing through the airline magazine stuck in the seat pocket in front of me (located right next to the "barf bag"). While glancing through it, I came upon an ad titled, "Mind Power Breakthrough." The sales pitch for this new machine was, "It's more than a cool way to relax after a hard day's work. It could be the most powerful learning tool since the invention of the book. Here's why. When you step into virtual reality your mind is cut off from any outside distractions. Your attention becomes focused inward as the powerful sensory stimulation bombards your imagination. Ideas and mental images float in and out of your consciousness. It feels like the best dream you've ever had, the most amazing thing you'll ever experience."

What a joke...can people be so blind as to spend one nickel on this gimmick? Our civilization in general wants to take a trip (mind) and never leave the farm. People are searching for a void-filler like a stray dog searches in alley way trash cans for a meal. Why? Why do we try everything in the gizmo books for *something* (instead of someone) to take us out of our pain and into someone else's (monetary) gain? Let me spell out the only "reality" that doesn't fade away or go out of style: J-E-S-U-S. Jesus is the medication for our pain, the answer to our questions, substance of our reality. Can we be so blind as to think that some contraption will free our conscious state, yet lock-up our emotions? Actual reality is that Christ is there for you and with you. Looking inward will land your spaced-out ship in a crater of despair. Blast off with Jesus and see just how far He will take you.

What do you think most people are searching for in this world that offers a "virtual reality" gimmick? How do people try to fill the void in their lives? What about you?

THRILLS YET SPILLS

Worldliness

"Do not love the world nor the things in the world, if anyone loves the world, the love of the father is not in him." 1 John 2:16

For years Disney theme parks have beguiled nearly three hundred and fifty million visitors (including Presidents, Hollywood stars, and foreign royalty) with their charismatic assortment of entertainment, spectacle, magic, and fantasy. The emphasis on adventure and thrills is unprecedented. For years these parks in southern California and Florida have been global leaders in adventure rides for all ages. The Matterhorn, Thunder Mountain, Star Wars, and the Jungle Cruise are big names in theme park rides. Each year, to stay on the cutting edge of technology, these parks open up a new ride or attraction to cast their nets for the American public's vacation dollar. Disney executives, "imagineers," builders, and technology experts mesh their talents with great minds like George Lucas (creator of *Indiana Jones* and *Star Wars* movies), and high-profile celebrities like Michael Jackson and Jim Henson (deceased mastermind of The Muppets).

Don't try to read between the lines here and conclude I'm down on Disney. I'm not. There is no greater place on this planet to spend a family vacation and your hard-earned dollar than one of these spectacular theme parks. My point is that the world is a lot like a theme park trying to lure you into a thrilling ride that can end up being a spectacular spill. This world has a lot to offer that may rob you of the riches of being a committed follower of Christ. The flash will soon fade and the sizzle go silent if you choose to indulge in its ways. Don't be fooled or taken in by the attractions of this world which will get you nowhere. These joy-rides don't let you off at the same place you entered in your life. They'll set you back, rough you up, bounce you around, then spit you out. Jesus' plans, on the other hand, are designed to be fun, yet safe as you commit to a ride which will take you into eternity. Now that's one ride that won't get old.

What does the world offer you that steals from you? Why is it so dangerous to ride the world's joy-rides? Has Jesus ever offered you or asked you to do anything that might harm you?

God the Father

"Know therefore that the Lord your God is God; He is the faithful God, keeping His covenant of love to a thousand generations of those who love him and keep his commands." Deuteronomy 7:9

Gladys Aylward, a missionary to China more than fifty years ago, was forced to flee when the Japanese invaded Yangcheng. She was so dedicated to her cause she just couldn't leave her work behind. With only one assistant, she led more than a hundred orphans over the mountains toward free China. In their book, *The Hidden Price of Greatness,* Ray Besson and Ranelda Hunsicker tell what happened:

During Gladys's harrowing journey out of a war-torn Yangcheng...she grappled with despair as never before. After passing a sleepless night, she faced the morning with no hope of reaching safety. A thirteen year old girl in the group reminded her of their much-loved story of Moses and the Israelites crossing the Red Sea.

"But I am not Moses," Gladys cried in desperation.

"Of course you aren't," the little girl replied, "but Jehovah is still God!"

The purpose of sharing this unique story is to illustrate a point which holds true some fifty years later. When Gladys and the orphans made it through to safety, they proved once again that no matter how inadequate we feel (don't let your feelings become facts), God is *still* God and we can trust in Him in every circumstance. I recall a friend telling me early in my life, "God doesn't call the qualified, He qualifies the called." Scripture logs a multitude of stories (true ones) that reveal just how involved God our Father is in each of our lives. You will be confronted with odds that seem overwhelming at a glance, but are peanuts to God. The same God of the Old Testament is still active and working today in lives and situations to provide a way to victory if we only trust Him. You don't have to "have it all together" or "be perfect" for God to use you in a situation that glorifies Him. God is in the business of pulling off miracles against all odds.

How big is God? Why is God so interested in you and your life that He even knows the number of hairs on your head? What does God ask from you to pull off a miracle? How deep is your faith and strong is your trust in Him? What could you do today to strengthen them?

AGAINST ALL ODDS

Set-Backs

"Tribulation brings forth perseverance." Romans 5:3

The car was a graduation gift, a 1960 Chevy with no radio or heater. That year, Jim Harrick drove it to Los Angeles where nobody even knew his name, bent on doing something big. Thirty-five years later, *Coach* Harrick of the UCLA Bruins returned to L.A. on a jet-liner with the whole town bowing down at his feet. The NCAA Final Four took place in Seattle Washington—UCLA Bruins up against the reining champs, Arkansas Razorbacks, on April 3, 1995. UCLA beat Arkansas 89-78 in the championship game. Despite the loss of point guard Tyus Edney, "the player who got us here," to an injured wrist in the semi-final game, they still grasped a title. This story would be just another sports blurb except for what happened in the locker room of the Bruins prior to tip-off. Ed O'Bannon (a senior) called a meeting of encouragement, but more importantly to pray for their attitude of not giving up and playing for God. With an opponent whose line-up included All-Americans like Scotty Thurman and Corliss Williamson, they realized they needed more than luck...they needed God. Bruins like Zidek, Bailey, and Ed's twin, Charles, turned in premier performances that ended in a national championship.

The reason I wanted to write of this game was not to just fill up space or highlight a great sports event. It was to illustrate with a modern day example how a set-back became a comeback. You *will,* I repeat, *will,* experience a multitude of set-backs in your life and then *you* have a decision to make...fish or cut bait, quit and give up, sink or swim. Hear this: it doesn't matter what has happened in your past, you, with God by your side (and in your prayers), can change the losing tradition into a winning record...just ask Coach Harrick.

What causes you to give up in certain situations? How can you learn from the 1995 National Championship UCLA Bruin team? Which is easier, to give up or push through a set-back? Why? Which do you do more often?

Prayer

"'Hear my prayer, O Lord, listen to my cry for help; be not deaf to my weeping. For I dwell with you as an alien, a stranger, as all my fathers were." Psalms 39:12

They all huddled in their yellow slickers while a deafening roar shook the ground like a herd of wild mustangs on a stampede. Six million gallons of water a minute burst over the falls in haphazard style. Onlookers were stricken with awe in the presence of such raw liquid power. For decades Niagara's "Maid of the Mist" has shuttled tourists safely to the brink of disaster for the sheer terror of being close to the source of power. No one who has ventured to this site will ever forget the experience.

Prayer should be like that. Drawing near to the source of life is indescribable. It's kinda' feeling safe and awestruck at the same time. Prayer, to this day, remains a ritual many speak about but few encounter personally. *US News and World Report* polled Americans about their spiritual lives, asking: "What best describes your beliefs about God?" 66% said God is a Father that can be reached by prayer, 11% said God is an idea, *not* a being, and 8% said God is an impersonal creator. Clearly, according to the results of this poll, Americans believe in prayer, yet the average believer spends less than two minutes a day doing it.

What prayer is *not*:

An occasional tourist excursion to the source of power.
A New Age feeling of oneness with Mother Earth.
A grocery list of "gimmies."
An alternative action.

What prayer *is:*

Abiding (resting) in God's presence.
Intimacy with the Father.
A personal relationship.
A warm embrace with God.
Attainable by all who believe.

Quote: "Anything that causes you to pray is a good thing."

What is the average amount of time per week you spend praying? What do you pray for? Why do you pray? What could help you to become a devout prayer warrior?

MENTORS

Leadership

"A pupil will eventually be like his teacher." Luke 6:40

A trusting mentor has a wide range of options for relating. He or she may counsel, teach, equip, guide, sponsor, or even coach. A good, effective mentor first has a servant's attitude and only offers wise counsel that chimes with scripture. The perception is that we *had* strong leaders in a past generation, but we have weak leaders today. Why? Where have all the leaders (mentors) gone? We can turn to Deuteronomy 31 and 34 to see how Moses passed the baton to Joshua, or to John 13 to see how Jesus himself was a mentor to his disciples by modeling servant leadership. Barnabas was a tremendous example of a person who lived for the next generation and not himself. We see how he spoke up for Saul who was the converted persecutor of Christians in Acts 9:26-31. Barnabus traveled to Tarsus to recruit Saul for a teaching role to the church in Antioch because he saw great potential. To be an effective mentor you must:

Believe in who you're discipling.

Serve as a team with them.

Part company and let them try on their own.

There are two rocks to avoid on your journey and that is to have all plans and no flexibility or have all flexibility and no plans.

Effective leading contains as its key ingredients directing, coaching, supporting, and delegating. You as the mentor need to be goal oriented. When the apostle Paul was a mentor to a younger Timothy, he did it through life-on-life, not via correspondence. Being a mentor is a hands-on process, not a step-back position. A mentor always provides an environment through encouragement and example that leads the follower to a deepened walk with the Savior. Hear this...being a mentor is not for cowards, but what is that's worth doing? The result of the effective mentor is that his disciple will continue the process with someone else after he's long gone.

Who is your mentor? Are you considered a mentor to anyone? Why or why not? Do you possess the tools it takes to be a hero to someone who needs one?

Love

"A fiend loves at all times." Proverbs 17:17

If you've ever been in a hospital to see someone in an intensive care unit, you'll appreciate this thought. The ICU waiting room is different from any place on our planet. The people who are waiting are different too. They can't do enough as they care for one another as servants. No one is selfish, rude, loud, or presumptuous. The distinction of race or social standards melt away like Popscicles on hot pavement. Everyone seems to pull for everyone else despite their differences. Vanity and pretense vanish. Minds and ears are focused on the doctor's next report. Everyone in the waiting room knows that loving someone else is what life and dreams are made of. Long before we are in an intensive care waiting room we should learn to love each other like our lives depend on it.

Why does it take a death or an extreme situation in our lives to make us show (and maybe even tell) some loved one that we really care about them. Life is too short and definitely too unpredictable to be walking around with the false belief that we have a lifetime to build on a valuable relationship. Jesus had three short years to mentor, love, disciple, and challenge His chosen twelve. He took His relationships seriously as He worked hard at developing their spiritual lives on a minute by minute scale. People, not programs are what make this world of chaos we live in go 'round. Begin to practice your intensive care for those few you call friend or loved one. Only one minute separates time from eternity...don't be late.

How are you on building relationships? Do you work on them or let them work on you? Who do you know today that could use a little intensive care? Give them a visit or call!

Anger

"Do not make friends with a hot-tempered man or you may learn his ways." Proverbs 22:24-25

There is a story told about ex-manager of the New York Yankees, Billy Martin, and baseball legend, Mickey Mantle, going on a hunting trip to Texas. Mickey had a friend who allowed them to hunt on his place, but asked them to check with the foreman of the ranch first. Upon their arrival Billy waited in the truck while Mickey checked in and told the foreman they had arrived. The foreman quickly gave permission, but asked for a small favor. The foreman had a pet plow mule that was going blind, but he didn't have the heart to put it out of misery, so he asked Mickey if he would mind shooting it. When Mickey was walking back to the truck, he decided to play a joke on Billy. He acted angry with the foreman and told Billy the foreman said they couldn't hunt and to get off of the property immediately. Mickey told Billy, "I'm gonna' show him. I'll just go and shoot one of the old man's mules." Billy said, "You're kidding! You can't do that." Mickey loaded his rifle, aimed at the blind mule standing in a nearby corral and pulled the trigger. Boom! Down went the mule, dead as a door nail. Before he had a chance to look up to see Billy's reaction, he heard two more loud booms (shots fired). Billy yelled out, "We'll show that son of a gun! I just killed two of his cows...let's go!"

Anger can be dangerously contagious. It infects those around us whether they know the source or reason(s) for our anger. The difference in our anger and Christ's anger is that they are at opposite ends of the spectrum. Christ's anger stemmed from lack of obedience to God's Word. Our anger *usually* is that of selfish desires and misconceptions. Be careful not to infect others with the virus of worldly anger. The consequences are more deadly than random gun-fire.

What ticks you off? Why is anger so destructive to relationships? How can you better take control of your anger in tense situations? How can we bridle our anger and use that energy in a more uplifting, constructive way?

Nature Of The Beast

Sin Nature

"Just as sin entered the world through one man, and death through sin, and in this way death came to all men, because all sinned." Romans 5:12

The famous cuckoo bird never builds its own nest. It searches for an unattended nest with eggs in it, lays its eggs there, then flies off. The thrush (the mother bird), whose nest has secretly been invaded, comes back, not noticing the new egg (lack of mathematical skills). What happens? Four thrushes hatch along with one large cuckoo chick, three times their size. When Mrs. Thrush brings home one large juicy worm for supper the cuckoo chick, being much larger and stronger, eats the entire meal with no leftovers for the smaller thrush chicks. The cuckoo bird gets bigger and bigger and the four thrushes get smaller and smaller. It's possible to walk along a hedgerow and find the dead thrushes a cuckoo bird has thrown out of the nest.

The apostle Paul teaches us that spiritually speaking, you've got two natures in one nest. The nature that you feed the most will grow the most and the nature you don't feed will end up starving to death. The nature that starves will diminish while the other takes charge of the nest (life). The way we feed our nature is through what we listen to, what we read, and how we ultimately think. Our theology and philosophy on practical living are directly related to who we are, our character. Maturity is the consistency between who we are when we are around others and when we are not. Our constant effort to renew our minds and mold our character are tied in with divine intervention. God is, and always will be, the only source of change from a state of destruction to a place of hope. Be careful what you feed in your life and make sure it's what you want to rule your roost (life).

What nature do you feed each day? How do you feed it? Is the wrong nature growing up in your life? What practical ways can you change this feeding pattern?

God's Love

"For God so loved the world" John 3:16

In a heart warming story, Mary Bird writes in her book, *The Whisper Test:*

I grew up knowing I was different, and hated it. I was born with a cleft palate (deformed mouth) and when I started school, my classmates made it clear to me how I looked to others: a little girl with a misshapen lip, crooked nose, lopsided teeth, and garbled speech. When schoolmates asked what happened to my lip I'd tell them I'd fallen and cut my lip on a piece of glass. Somehow it seemed more acceptable to have suffered on accident than to have been born different. I was convinced that no one outside my family could love me. There was, however, a teacher in the second grade whom we all adored—Mrs. Leonard. She was short, round, happy, and a sparkling lady. Annually we had a hearing test that Mrs. Leonard gave to all the students and finally it was my turn. I knew from past years that as we stood against the door in the back of the room and covered one ear, the teacher would whisper something like "the sky is blue" or "do you have new shoes?" and we would have to repeat it back. I waited there for those words that God must have put into her mouth, those seven words that changed my life. Mrs. Leonard said in her whisper, "I wish you were my little girl.

Wow! God says to every person that is deformed by sin or poor self-image, "I wish you were my child." We can't even comprehend with our feeble minds the love that Christ has for us...for you! He loved you so much that He was willing to risk it all for a chance to have a relationship with you. God is *not* as concerned with *what* we do as *who* we are. I'm telling you that you may feel like a total failure, an outcast, a misfit, a geek, but God doesn't see it that way. God created you from the beginning of time and He doesn't make junk.

How do you feel today about yourself? Can you relate with this story? Are you happy with the way you look? Does God love you?

HAZARDS

Trials

"Happy is the man who perseveres under trial, for once he has survived, he will receive the crown of life." James 1:12

Life, like the game of golf, is full of hazards. If you've ever lost your senses and attempted to pick up the goofy game of golf, then this devotional will make a lot of sense. If you haven't gone crazy yet and tested your patience at this game of cow-pasture pool, then you're way ahead of the game. Golf, like few sports, is a game that can turn a tender, compassionate, easy-going individual into a schizophrenic, psychopathic club-slinger. I've often asked myself, "Self, why should it be so difficult to put a little white dimpled ball into a cup stuck out in the middle of a slab of grass (the green)? Why is it so hard to swing a metal club in such a manner as to strike that stupid ball and cause it to project in the direction you aimed it?" Answer: who knows and who cares! I quit!

For as long as I can remember I have had a club in my hand and golf shoes on my feet. My father and I today still enjoy (to use the word loosely) going to the links and playing eighteen holes. After giving it my best for thirty years, to this day I spend more time behind trees, in bushes, in sand traps, and on cart paths than I do in the middle of a lush, green, groomed fairway. I know I'm slow, but I finally came to the realization that in life, hazards are just a part of the game. Think about it...difficulties like trials, snares, and pitfalls, just like water, trees, rough, rocks, and sand traps are what make the game (life or golf) fun! That's right, *fun*! You have a choice, either run from difficulties (you can't hide) or embrace them as part of the game. You will find yourself excited about your growing and deepening faith when trials come rolling your way. God uses trials to strengthen your game so that you can enjoy life to the fullest. Life, unlike the game of golf, is designed to be fun and fulfilling...golf on the other hand is designed to be frustrating and trying. Go ahead, tee it up and take a swing at it...just watch the hazards.

What hazards do you hate to face? Do you see them as a positive part of your life or an inconvenience? What would happen if you viewed them as a plus instead of a minus?

Goals

"As for me and my house, we will serve the Lord." Joshua 24:15

Every effective ministry I'm aware of has a statement of purpose in their material somewhere. A mission statement is a key ingredient in getting from point 'A' to point 'B' in a ministry. I am amazed how the organizations that don't have a mission statement make it, even for one year. The purpose of a mission statement is:

To direct.

To maintain a distinct purpose.

To hold accountable.

To assign a calling.

To deputize a task.

As you can plainly see...this way of attaining a specific goal isn't limited to Christian ministries. In fact—does your family have a mission statement? Why not? The first place we need these guidelines in place is with our families. What an awesome way to show to a community of friends and associates the direction your family is headed. Mission statements are useful tools for checking out other church and para-church organizations. They provide a window to the philosophy and theology of the group.

A mission statement should be a lot like an advertising slogan. Nike's "Just Do It" was a huge hit because it says so much in so few words. In the same way, a mission statements should make a point without being wordy. My personal guide is to say what needs saying in twenty words or less—that makes you think through what you want to communicate. Use direct, targeted words, not cliché or general terms. Make your mission statement a community of goals that can be used to direct your ship.

Write out your own personal mission statement in twenty words or less. Sit down with your family after supper and write out a family mission statement, frame it, and put it in your family room. Review this statement monthly and evaluate how you're doing personally and as a family.

Believe You...Me

Trusting

"Glory to God in the highest, and on earth, peace among men with whom I am well pleased." Luke 2:14

One of the greatest story-lines ever placed in a film can be found in the movie *Hook.* Robin Williams played a "success-driven" father who desired to love his family, but was caught up in the corporate scene. His children ran away to the fantasy world of "Neverland" to look for happiness, but ran into "Captain Hook" (played by Dustin Hoffman). The children's father became Peter Pan in search of his kidnapped kids, along with his trusty side-kick, "Tinker Bell," played by none other than Julia Roberts. Pete and Tinker teamed up with a ruddy band of young brigades to bring down "Hook" and his not-so-merry men. In the climax, Peter Pan and Captain Hook faced each other in a final duel of swords. At one point during the fight, it looked as if Hook would be victorious. Peter seemed without hope, until...his grungie brigade of boys quietly began to chant, "I believe in you...Peter, I believe in you." This gave Peter a sudden burst of energy and new-found confidence to ultimately defeat Hook, return to reality, and become a great dad.

I enjoyed this movie most, not because of the Academy Award acting or special effects, but for the one punch line, "I believe in you." What an awesome transformation occurs when we're told that someone out there believes in us. God said of Jesus, "This is my Son with whom I am well pleased." The flip side of this statement shows how to believe in someone else (verbally). There is no mountain you can't climb or tough time you can't overcome knowing that someone believes in you. Being believed in is just one step beneath being told you're loved. In fact, they should go together like peas and carrots (a *Forrest Gump* line). Show your confidence, support, and trust, in someone today by telling them you believe in them...start with your Savior first.

Who was the last person you told, "I believe in you?" Who has said they believe in you? Does God believe in you? How do you know? Go tell someone!

Planting Prayers

Prayer

"And this I pray, that your love may abound still more and more..." Philippians 1:9

Elzeard Bouffier was one of those people I wish lived in our day in time. He was a shepherd in the French Alps at a time when people were cutting down trees left and right in the mountains around Provence, France. After supper each night, the shepherd sorted through a pile of acorns, throwing away those that were small or cracked. For over three years, while herding and watching his sheep on the barren mountainsides, he planted these acorns and eventually planted around 100,000, 20,000 of which sprouted. He expected half to be eaten by animals or die due to the elements, but the rest to live. After World War I, the mountainside blossomed with acorn trees. In an ecology sheltered by a leafy roof and bonded to the earth by a mat of roots, willow rushes, meadows, gardens, and flowers were birthed. The shepherd, ignoring the war of 1939 just as he had ignored the war in 1914, continued his planting on other barren mountains. The streams, fed by the rains and snows that the forest conserves, are flowing healthier today than ever before, due to one man's quest.

People who are prayer warriors are like spiritual reforesters, digging holes in a barren land and planting the seeds of life. Through these seeds, the dry spiritual wastelands are transformed into harvestable fields, and life-giving water is brought to parched and barren souls of the lost. You have a responsibility as a Christian, as did the shepherd, to replant your prayers in this barren, ugly, world. God has given each of us an incredible opportunity to commune (talk and listen) with the Creator and petition needs (not wants) for yourself and others. Take the time out of each busy day to plant a prayer, then sit back and watch it grow into a miraculous answer.

How often do you pray? How can you become a more diligent prayer warrior? Take a minute right now to pray for your needs and others' souls.

Christian Walk

"And God is able to make all grace abound to you, so that in all things at all times, having all that you need, you will abound in every good work." 2 Corinthians 9:8

How many fans do you think would follow a team that came out each night and played to lose? Let me give you a clue...zippo, the big goose egg, nil, nada! The world needs to see folks who are winning in their walk with Christ. The following is a poetic list of tips to help you win in your walk with Jesus:

Don't take too long—
to admit when you are wrong!

"If we claim to be without sin, we deceive ourselves and the truth is not in us." 1 John 1:8

Identify, confess, and forget your sin—
He died on the cross so you could win!

"If we confess our sins, He is faithful and just and will forgive us our sins and purify us from all righteousness. If we claim to be without sin, we made Him out to be a liar, and His work has no place in our lives." 1 John 1:9-10

You can overcome anything—
if your faith is in the King.

"I tell you the truth, no one can see the kingdom of God unless he is born again." John 3:3 "Therefore, if anyone is in Christ, he is a new creation. The old has gone, the new has come!" 2 Corinthians 5:17

To avoid a mental riot—
get alone with God and be quiet!

"Do not be anxious about anything, but in everything by prayer and petition, with thanksgiving, present your requests to God, and the peace of God, which transcends all understanding, will guard our hearts and your minds in Christ Jesus." Philippians 4:6-7

Read your Bible every day—
or soon there might be hell to pay!

"For the Word of God is living and active, sharper than any double-edged sword, it penetrates, even to dividing soul and spirit, joints and marrow, it judges the thoughts and attitudes of the heart." Hebrews 4:12

(continued on next page)

Every single day—
take the time to pray.

"Be joyful always, pray continually, give thanks in all circumstances for this is God's will for you in Christ Jesus." 1 Thessalonians 5:16

To set your heart and mind on things above—
concentrate on building your ladder of love.

"Since then, you have been raised with Christ, set your hears on things above, where Christ is seated at the right hand of God. Set your minds on things above, not on earthly things."

The law of the harvest you must know—
you'll eventually reap the seeds that you sow.

"Do not be deceived, God cannot be mocked. A man reaps what he sows. The one who sows to reap his sinful nature, from that nature will reap destruction. The one who sows to please the Spirit, from the Spirit will reap eternal life." Galatians 6:7

Take daily action to communicate—
write, call, encourage—love in action is great!

"In the same way, faith, by itself, is not accompanied by action, is dead." James 2:17

Do not get entangled in worldly affairs—
keeping things simple will limit your cares.

"No soldier in active service entangles himself in the affairs of everyday life, so that he may please the one who enlisted him as the soldier." 2 Timothy 2:4

No matter how deep you are in the hole—
remember that God is still in control.

"At once I was in the spirit, and there before me was a throne with someone sitting on it!" Revelations 4:2

Conclusion:

When Jesus hung on a cross atop the city dump, it signified the victory we (you) have at our fingertips, with Him as our coach. Be a beacon of light in a dark, lost world that exemplifies just how abundant and down-right fun a life with Christ can be!

Share the list above with your family around the supper table tonight. Talk about each verse.

A Sales Pitch

Being Honest

"Behold, an Israelite indeed, in who there is no guile!" John 1:4 Note: This is what Christ said of Nathaniel.

If you're anything like me, the first thing you look for when you open up the daily newspaper is the comic strips. In the classroom setting of one of the "Peanuts" comics, it was the first day of school, and the students were asked to write an essay about returning to school. Lucy wrote, "Vacations are nice, but it's good to get back to school. There is nothing quite as satisfying as a good education and I look forward to a new year of expanding my knowledge." The teacher was very impressed and complimented Lucy on the essay. Lucy then leaned over to Charlie Brown and said, "After a while, you learn what sells."

I remember this particular comic well because it reminds me of how we may respond to others in our walk with Christ. The temptation may be to say what people *want* to hear, whether it's the truth or not. When we compromise our message, we sell the integrity of our soul. Integrity is one of those qualities that can only exist with divine intervention. When we sell ourselves out and tarnish our integrity with deceit and lies, we lose. Integrity is like the western spotted owl—an endangered species. Few people possess this quality that sets a Christian apart from those who don't know Christ. Truth, whether you see much of it or not, is the best standard to live by. Don't sell yourself out to the temptation to be accepted, be cool, or be "in," by being one way in church and another way in school, work, or on the playing field. What sells usually smells!

Do others consider you to be a person of truth? Do you sell out around your peers? What temptations overtake you to sell out to a lie? Why are truth and integrity so important to a Christian in today's market?

Our Tongue

"He who guards his mouth and his tongue keeps himself from calamity." Proverbs 21:23

I love the Christmas season and all that goes with it. There is nothing quite like all the festive rituals, gift, and TV specials which all tend to set us in a festive mood. *A Christmas Story,* the classic movie, is a nostalgic look at a boy growing up in the midwestern town of Gary, Indiana. In one memorable scene we find Ralphy (the boy) at a recess in school in the middle of winter. Two boys, surrounded by their classmates, argue whether a person's tongue will stick to a metal pole in below-freezing weather. Eventually, one of the boys folds under peer pressure and a "triple-dog dare," and sticks his tongue on the frigid metal flagpole. Sure enough, it gets stuck and the bell rings to begin class again. Everyone, including the boy who made the dare, runs into the school building, leaving one sucker stuck to the pole. The teacher asks where the absent student is and then looks out the school window to see the boy in pain with his tongue frozen to the pole.

Now, I realize this is a little extreme, but I want to make a valid point. Though few of us are brainless enough to get into this kind of predicament, we *do* let our tongues get us in trouble. When *we* (you) suffer the pain that eventually recoils on everyone who speaks boastful words, lies, bitter or cruel words, hypocritical or doubting words, we learn the truth of the proverb at the top of this page. Guard—literally guard—your tongue like a wild prisoner and don't allow it to escape and cause trouble in someone's life. Sticks and stones will break your bones, but words can do much worse. Tie up your tongue, except to encourage or speak God's truth.

What is gossip? Is it of Satan or God? How much trouble does a loose tongue cause? Do you use your tongue as a weapon? Why? How can you realistically guard your tongue so it won't hurt someone? Make today a day in which your tongue does nothing but encourage others.

Friendship

"Carry each other's burdens, and in this way you will fulfill the law of Christ." Galatians 6:2

Mr. Alter's fifth grade class at Lake Elementary School in Oceanside, California, included fourteen bald-headed boys. Only one had no choice in the matter. Ian O'Gorman was losing his hair in clumps as the result of the chemotherapy used to fight lymphoma. So Ian wouldn't feel out of place in the classroom, all thirteen of his buddies shaved their heads too. If they all were bald, no one could point out the one who had cancer. A ten-year-old boy named Kyle started it all as he proposed the plan to the group, then marched them all down to the barber. Ian's father, touched by the gesture of compassion, was in tears as he told them how he appreciated their kindness and good deed.

What an awesome example of carrying a burden for a friend. You don't often see such a sense of compassion. Take a look sometime at the words that precede an act of healing by Jesus in the gospels. They state, "He felt compassion, so...." So what? Sew buttons on your underwear? No. So, He did something about it by expressing empathy for the afflicted and became part of the solution, not the problem. There is probably no better way to show how much Jesus you have living in your heart than by carrying someone else's burden(s). Our second greatest commandment is, "Love your neighbor as yourself." Do you realize just how much you love yourself? Let me answer that, and I don't even know you...*a lot!* Tune in to the spirit of Christ and see where He leads you and what cross (burden) He leads you to carry for a friend. You'll feel good about yourself and this selfish world will know that you are different.

How compassionate are you? Have you ever acted on that sense? Why or why not? Who could you help today? What are you waiting on?

Life In The 90's

Person of Christ

"Be still and know that I am God." Psalm 46:10

If you feel like you really are a person of the 90's and on the fast-track, then you probably see your life something like this:

Your life passes you by at 90 miles an hour.
You end up working 90 hours a week.
Your to-do list has 90 items on it.
You're on a 90 calorie a day diet because you're 90 pounds overweight.
You have at least 90 bills to pay each month.
Your bank account is $90 overdrawn.
The minimum payment on your credit card is $90 (and that's just interest).
You'll be paying off student loans for 90 more months.
You don't know where you'll get $90,000 (each) to send your kids to college.
Your TV has 90 cable channels and there's nothing good to watch.
You have 90 different activities to attend each week.
Your car just rolled over 90,000 miles.
You just answered the phone for the 90th time today.
The cheapest pair of tennis shoes you can find cost $90.
Life would be just grand if you only made $90,000 more a year.

Life in the 90's is definitely not all it's cracked up to be. It seems the faster you run, the further you lag behind, the days get shorter, while the list of things to do gets longer. Our lives get tangled in a web that can soon strangle us. We get so involved with our busy agenda that we lose sight of our purpose. God is not as concerned with what we *do,* as who we *are* in Christ. Take time away from the rat-race to *be still* and take quiet refuge with your Creator. You'll never cope with the agenda of the 90's until you tank-up with God for your fuel each day. Take a time-out and re-group.

How busy are you? Are you too busy for God? When was the last time you were still? Do you meet with God in your stillness? When and where can you be still for thirty minutes a day to meet with your Savior in prayer and meditation?

THE RACE

Christian Walk

"I have fought the good fight, finished the race and I have kept the faith." 2 Timothy 4:7

It took place at the NCAA cross-country championship held in Riverside, California, when 123 out of the 128 runners took the same wrong turn. One competitor, Mike Delcavo, stayed on course and tried waving for fellow runners to follow him. He was only able to convince four runners to stay on the right course with him—everyone else followed the crowd. Asked what his competitors thought of his mid-race decision to use his own judgment instead of following the crowd, Delcavo responded, "They thought it was funny that I went the right way."

In the same way, our goal as Christians is to run correctly and finish the race that has been marked out for us. We can celebrate with those few runners in this Christian race who have enough courage to ignore the laughter and tongue-lashings of the watching world, stay on track, and finish. This race we (you) are called to run is not a hundred yard dash...it's the marathon of life. You see, we don't need much training to finish a sprint, but to finish a race where we can't see the finish line from the start (like a marathon) we need a Savior. I have personally run only a half marathon (thirteen miles) and thought *it* was gonna' kill me. I can only imagine running two or three hours (for me it would take two or three days) for twenty-six miles. I get tired just driving that far, much less using my legs to get me there. The race God has called us to run takes:

Daily training in the Word of God
Faith in our Lord
Discipline to follow the course, not the crowd
Stamina to persevere in tough times
Love as our carbo-load fuel

Finish well!

Are you swayed by others to take a course in life other than the one laid out by Christ? Is it important to finish our Christian race? Why? Who ultimately gets all the glory?

Example of Christ

"Show yourself an example of those who believe." 1 Timothy 4:12

There's an interesting account of a lady named Judy Anderson, who grew up as the daughter of a missionary in Zaire. As a little girl, she went to a day-long rally celebrating the one hundredth anniversary of Christian missionaries coming to Zaire. After a long day of speeches and festive music, an old man came out of the crowd and insisted that he be allowed to speak. He told the crowd that he soon would die and that he alone had some important information to share. He explained that when the missionaries came one hundred years before, his people thought they were strange and their message unusual. The tribal leaders decided to test the missionaries by slowly poisoning them to death. Over a period of months and years, all the missionaries and their families died one by one. The old man said, "It was as we watched *how* they died that we decided we wanted to live as Christians."

That story had gone untold for a hundred years. Those faithful followers died and never knew why they were dying. They stayed true to their tasks and loyal to their Lord, not knowing what an impact, even to their last few breaths, they made on thousands of viewers who saw Christ in the crisis. You don't have to be in Africa or a missionary for folks to see the Christ in you. It's easy to be a Christian during those high times, but what about when you're in the valleys of life? Are you gonna' be one of those followers who takes Christ with you, even to your grave? I hope and pray so!

Do people see Christ in the middle of your crisis? How much impact does your every reaction have on others? How many eyes watch you even though you're not aware of them?

Crowd Barriers

Peer Pressure

"He was trying to see who Jesus was, and he was unable because of the crowd, for he was small in stature. He climbed up in a sycamore tree in order to see Him." Luke 19:4-5

This is a great story and a window for learning more about what's needed to follow Christ. This particular story is about a rich, little tax-gatherer who one day woke up to the sounds of multitudes and went to see what all the commotion was about. Zaccheus had evidently heard of Jesus, yet hearing wasn't necessarily believing. Old Zack (we'll call him that for short because I get tired of writing his whole name out) was no different from the "groupies" that migrate from town to city following rock bands, super-star athletes, or Hollywood heroes. Zack wanted to catch a glimpse of this man who some claimed to be God and others claimed to be a pest. No matter what the papers and tabloids were saying, he just had to get a "look-see" for himself. The only problem with the pursuit of his dream was that there were too many people in his way. Now, I don't know if he was a bona fide pigmy, or just shorter than average, but a ground-floor view just wasn't cuttin' it. So, creative genius that he was, he reverted back to his childhood days and scaled the nearest sycamore tree for a bird's-eve view of the man from Nazareth.

The lesson today, students, deals with barriers. That's right...those walls of worldliness that seem to park it right in front of our view of the Savior. It seems to my recollection that often the barrier comes in the form of people. People, secular and Christian, can step right in your way to block your path for following Jesus. People of any shape, form, height, or religion can blockade you from a relationship with Christ. Do whatever it takes to see Jesus daily (climb a tree) and continue your growth process. I'd imagine from Zack's perspective, it's a view worth fighting for.

What barriers come between you and Christ? How do you get around, over, or under them? How much sacrifice do you go through to see the Savior? Are you willing to be different and climb a few trees?

STEPPIN' OUT

Faith

"And He said 'Come' and Peter stepped out of the boat and walked on the water and came toward Jesus." Matthew 14:29

Have you ever been summoned to step out before? How about at a track meet when the coach tells you, before the final race, to step out? What about when a friend encourages you to step out of your comfort zone and try something different? How about on the dance floor? When does someone describes you as steppin' out of your normal ways and doing something totally out of character?

I love the story of Peter (the disciple) being scared from sailing in the storm. He looked off the port side (just a guess) and saw someone apparently walking on top of the rough seas. Don't you know he rubbed his red eyes and did a double take? It was at that moment he realized it was his hero, Jesus, and then he was asked to come along for a casual walk on the water. Sure! Right! Can't you just hear old Pete saying to himself, "Jesus, you must be crazy...me, walk on that water? I don't think so."

The ending to this scene in scripture is worth reading again. Peter, Mr. Aggressive, jumped out of the boat (his comfort zone), and began walking on the water toward Jesus. He must have felt pretty powerful and cool until that moment he took his focus off Christ. Reality set in and when he looked down he began to sink like a brick. I'm not sure about this, but I'll bet ya' that Peter was no All-American swimmer and wondered if he wasn't about to become shark bait.

Jesus calls us daily to walk away from security blankets and step out in faith to follow Him. Walking on water is not easy, but neither is having total faith in the Master's plans. Faith is the assurance of things hoped for (fear of not drowning) and the conviction of things not seen (waves of turbulent tough times). Go ahead...step out. Jesus won't let you sink.

Has God ever called you to step out of your comfort zone and do something totally radical for Him? Why is it so tough to step-out on unsure waters and follow him? When will you step out of your boat?

Death

"There is a way that seems right to a man, but it ends in sudden death." Proverbs 16:25

There are two arenas of conversation where you'll find the term, "sudden death." One is the sports arena, and the other is life. We love it in the first context and fear it in the other. It's not a subject fondly looked upon at a party or during dinner, yet it's destined to become reality in both circles. Death, or even the thought of it, runs a chill up one's spine. It's been said in a world of uncertainty, there are only two absolutes—death and taxes. The older you get the clearer this will become. The funny thing (sorry about my choice of words) about dying is that *it* really isn't the deciding time...it's just the final chapter. But once a person passes through those doors, we never hear from them what's on the other side. So we must rely on the "faith factor."

My question to you is this...where are you going? Death is swift, sudden, sad, yet very real. You *will* die and either spend eternity in torment and torture, or paradise and peace. The decisions and choices that you make today will affect your ultimate destiny. My suggestion to you, no matter how long you think you may live (no guarantees) or how comfortable you might become, is that you take a good hard look at yourself and see who is gonna' win in your sudden death. Side note: Don't think for a moment that you're gonna' take your worldly possessions with you to comfort you. Have you ever seen a U-Haul behind a hearse?

If you were to die a sudden death today, where would your new residence be?

MR. NICE GOD

Deity

"'I am the Alpha and the Omega,' says the Lord God, 'who is and who was and is to come, the Almighty.'" Revelations 1:8

A French philosopher once wrote, "God made man in His own image, and man returned the favor." Ever since sin entered the garden and ruined that perfect image, we (Christian society) have been trying to recreate God. We want a god we can comprehend in neat, finite, human terms. We want a deity we can understand, predict, and figure out. In The Temple of the Thousand Buddhas, a place of worship in Japan, the followers design their own god. This temple is filled with a thousand likenesses of Buddha, each different from the next. Worshipers pick and choose which likeness of god they prefer. Isn't this a bit like some Christians today whose search for the "quick fix" leads to a religious compromise. We have given God a "modern day make-over" at the expense of reverence for His sovereignty. We have made Him a "user friendly" pal—a God who makes allowances for our sin and excuses for our unholy behavior, a non-judgmental God who will fit right in to our lifestyle and give us "brownie points" for doing a good job.

Martin Lloyd-Jones said, "People who teach that God is love without teaching that He *hates* sin are presenting another god—essentially Satan with a mask on." The hottest selling books in Christian bookstores are the touchy-feely type that focus on self-esteem, self-fulfillment, and self-analysis. Books that encourage self-sacrifice are the ones gathering dust or out of print, yet are what we need to be reading (along with the Bible). A 1994 *US News and World Report* cover story on spirituality states, "American religion has taken on the aura of pop psychology. Many congregations have multiplied their membership by going light on theology and offering worshipers a steady diet of sermons and support groups that emphasize personal fulfillment." Folks are giving the Bible a make-over and revising the Lord's Prayer to say, "Our Father and Mother who art in heaven...." Give me a break! God is God! Don't forget...it's Christ who changes us—not the other way around.

Who is God to you? Do you try to change Him? Don't!

The Transfusion

God's Love

"Walk in love, just as Christ also loved you, and gave Himself up for us, and offering and a sacrifice to God as a fragrant aroma." Ephesians 5:2

In old westerns, the town "Doc" carried his little black bag from home to home via horse and buggy, making house-calls to all the area residents. This is the true story of Dr. Cain, a small town doctor from the midwest in 1910. Dr. Cain received word that a six-year-old girl had suffered a severed artery and was bleeding to death. He raced to the scene, as does a modern day paramedic (except he was on horseback). After applying direct pressure and stitches, he had the bleeding controlled, but the girl had lost too much blood and would soon die. Dr. Cain knew her only hope was a transfusion, yet in that day and time, this practice was just that...a practice. The little girl's ten-year-old brother overheard the conversation between the doctor and his parents, and quickly volunteered his services as a donor. After a successful transfusion, the boy lay shaking on the table next to his sister. The doctor asked, "Son, why are you shaking?" The boy replied, "Doctor, *when* am I gonna' die?"

What an awesome visual picture of what Jesus did for you and me. The little boy *thought* he had given all his blood so that his sister might live. Jesus *did* die for you and me. Sacrificial love is something we don't often find. It seems that most people are out to see how much they can get, not give. The premier example of sacrifice took place on Calvary two thousand years ago as our Creator in the punished flesh, hung to die between two criminals. Be a follower who is ready to volunteer his life for the cause of Christ.

When you hear the word sacrifice what do you think about? Is it worldly or divine? Are you *really* willing to lay down your life for Jesus daily? What's stopping you?

THE HUNT

Easter

"So the other disciple who had first come to the tomb entered then also, and he saw and believed." John 20:8

I wasn't quite sure if I was attending a concert or an early morning Easter service. The location was "Fiddler's Green," and the attendance was somewhere around ten thousand. It was an outdoor amphitheater and you couldn't have painted a more beautiful day or a more scenic backdrop than the Colorado Rockies (and I don't mean the baseball team). I was amazed at the number that showed up, yet I question some motivations for attendance. Did they come because of ritual, guilt, status, or conviction, or was it for celebration? Well...only God knows, but the worship service was awesome.

Easter is far more than a time to hunt for colored, hard-boiled eggs or dress up in a festive new outfit. It's above all the hype, yet down to earth enough to understand. Easter is the celebration following Good Friday which separates the Christian from Ala or Mohammed. You see, those who worship *another* god, honor a dead god that didn't die specifically for them. We get so excited about the empty tomb, yet our future lies in a risen Lord. When Peter and the other disciples saw the empty tomb, they realized what Mary knew as she sat outside the tomb and wept. As believers in Christ, we don't worship a grave, bronze statue, or a past legend, but a risen, living, breathing, omnipresent God. Now, if that thought doesn't get your blood flow movin,' then I'm not sure you are alive (take a moment and check your pulse). Gang, who gives a rip about the tomb? He's alive!!!

Why should you be more excited about a living Jesus than an empty tomb? Why is it so important to our faith that we worship and follow a L-I-V-I-N-G Savior? Talk amongst yourselves.

God

"Jesus replied, 'Love the Lord your God with all your heart and with all your soul and with all your mind.'" Matthew 22:37

"Whatever it takes to get their attention," is the motto of the ad agencies. The competition is getting so fierce, so dog-eat-dog, that they will try just about any shock method to stimulate the viewer to purchase. The Independent Media Network based in London, England, was the first to set the perverted pace as they allowed new shock ads to be aired on TV. They showed horse corpses falling two stories, transvestites in cabs, topless women, bondage, mock sex, and to top it off, dismembered body parts. The point is that the folks who are *supposed* to be screening these ads have instead bought into the hype. Now, you might be saying, "Hey, that's in London, not Dallas," but I'm saying it's on its way to good ol' America in just a matter of time.

Our human (sinful) nature is and always will be on the fast track to hell if we let it take its natural course. The TV is gonna' get worse, the domestic violence, the chemical abuse, killing of babies, homosexual activity, disease...need I go on? Jesus is the one and only answer to our problems, whether here or abroad, via media or on the streets, in the clinics or in the hospitals. Our love (passion) must be for God Almighty and not for the newest style or latest car. Our love must first be for God, above the opposite sex, career placement, or dollar bills. Come on, "Holmes," how tough is it to see that *without* Him we crater and *with* Him we climb? This devo, I'm sure, is not a revelation in Calvinistic Theology, but it is an attempt to get you off your content behinds, and on your faithful knees. Loving God is *not* a one time decision that lasts forever...it's should be renewed daily.

Do you really love God? How much? When? For how long? Daily? Weekly? Monthly? How about lifely (is that a word)?

Broken Spirit

"Simon, Simon, behold, Satan has demanded permission to sift you like wheat," Luke 22:31

Take a moment to read in your Bible the verses prior to this one, beginning at verse 24. Do you see it? Do you see a gold nugget of scripture? What rich verses, full of knowledge and wisdom! We are all trying to make it to the top. We are all striving after a goal or reward that we think (false security) might fill the void in the pit of our stomachs. The problem is that to go up we must first go down, to win we must lose, to gain we must die...be sifted. The word sifted means to be separated, strained, screened, and sorted out (doesn't sound like fun). If you think about it for a minute, there are only three thing we bring to the table—time, talent, and treasure. That's it. No more, no less. Today we are either building upon *our* kingdom or God's kingdom. When we build on ourselves, we show the world statues in our memory, trophies accepted on our behalf. What is amazing about these treasures of self is that we aren't going to take them with us in eternity. God treasures those who are selfless, those who leave behind a Godly heritage, not an inheritance. Here is a little insight...you will not build a treasure for God until you have been "sifted" like wheat. Why? Because the process of sifting out self includes pain and suffering. Sifting is good for our maturing process and can only be accomplished by a divine God who knows what needs to be sifted out of our spiritual lives. Dying to self is a long, hard, process, but worth it when it comes to harvesting a good product.

What are your talents? How are you using them today? Who gets the credit? Have you ever been sifted before? Was it a good or bad experience? Why or why not? What selfish desires do you think God needs to sift out of your life before He will use you?

THANKSGIVING FEAST

Being Thankful

"Let the peace of Christ rule in your hearts, to which you were called in one body and be thankful." Colossians 3:15

One of the least used phrases in the English language is "thank you." As the father of three bone-headed boys, I can personally testify that they would much rather say things like "no" and "mine."

The Masai tribe in West Africa has a very unusual way of saying thank you. Translators tell us that when the Masai express thanks, they bow, put their forehead on the ground, and essentially say, "My head is in the dirt." When members of another African tribe want to express their gratitude and appreciation, they sit for a long time in front of the hut of the person who did them a favor and literally say, "I sit on the ground before you."

These Africans demonstrate well the meaning of true thanksgiving. At the core is a sincere act of humility and grace. Even Jesus must have been disappointed when He healed the ten lepers of their skin disease and only one returned to say thank you. Why is it so difficult to utter those two simple words to our parents, friends, God, and anyone who deserves them? Being gracious and courteous requires maturity and wisdom. Why do we need a holiday each year to remind us to be thankful? Humble yourself (it's gonna' take an act of God to pull it off) *today*, go to those who have sacrificed for you and give them the greatest gift...a thank you. Look them in the eye, give them a sincere hug (no handshakes) and humbly say thank you for all they've done for you. Be like the one leper who treasured his gift and returned his appreciation.

When was the last time you said thank you? Why is it so hard? Do you have an attitude of humility when you say thank you? Make it a point today to say thank you at least twenty times to your teachers, parents, coaches, friends, and gas station attendants. When you pray tonight thank God.

Sharing Christ

"Preach the word, be ready in and out of season, reprove, rebuke, exhort with great patience and instruction." 2 Timothy 4:2

In 1992, a Los Angeles county parking control officer came upon an El Dorado Cadillac illegally parked next to the curb on street-sweeping day. The officer wrote out a ticket, ignoring the man in the driver's seat, reached inside the open window, and placed the thirty dollar citation on the dashboard. The driver made no excuse for his poor parking, no argument ensued—and with good reason. He was dead. The driver had been shot in the back of the head twelve hours before, but was sitting up, stiff as a board with blood running down his back. The officer was so preoccupied with his duties that he was unaware of anything out of the ordinary. He got back in his patrol car and drove away.

What an incredible example and lesson to us all to slow down from our fast paced lives and take the time to share Christ with those who are dead in their sins. What should catch our attention most is their need, not their offenses. We, as Christians, get so caught up in judging others' offenses that we lose our focus and purpose. They don't need a citation, they need a Savior. Your goal as a Christian is that when you die, you take along as many souls with you as possible. Sharing Christ with someone is not an A+B=C formula...it's original and fueled by the Holy Spirit. An effective evangelist is sincere, obedient to the Spirit, a good listener, a question-asker, and tender in approach. Granted, some are better than others, but we can all get out there and practice.

Are you so busy with your Christian duty that you lose sight of your purpose? When was the last time you shared Christ with a (spiritually) dead person? Are you scared to? Why? Go with a pastor or any older Christian one night this month and share Christ with someone.

That's Unreal

God

"For I am mindful of the sincere faith within you." 2 Timothy 1:5

"Unreal!" This exclamation is sometimes used to punctuate a certain event in history, a sports spectacle, or even a monumental task. When something is described as unreal, it may then be compared to something that *is* real. Reality is a term used widely today to describe a fact, a definite situation, the here and now. To be unreal, the situation is therefore placed out-of-reach, as in a mirage or an illusion. What am I blabbering about? Take this thought and put it in the bank. There are far too many supposed followers of Christ who aren't concentrating on the marching orders foretold in the Bible. Our lost culture needs to see a "realness" in our faith and a touchable God. A relationship with Christ is not a group commitment...it's personal. Not so personal that we keep it to ourselves and never share it with anyone else, but real. I believe that by our own lifestyle we paint the picture of one of two things...either a God who created all that exists, or an "unreal," untouchable God who only shows up in pictures on the Sunday school bulletin boards. Abba Father must be real in our lives and a reality in our hearts. God is *not* some fairy tale fable that only existed in the long-ago. Yes, God is hard to imagine when it comes to things like creating an entire universe or making the dead live again. He did come in a real earth-suit to live, breath, sweat, cry, bleed, laugh, avoid temptation, suffer pain, and die like a criminal. But, but, but...He rose in seventy-two hours to become reality in our hearts and save us from eternal torment in hell—if we choose to believe. God only becomes "unreal" when we don't get real with Him.

How real is God to you? When does He seem to be unreal? If your friends were to determine if God is real or unreal in your life, what would they say?

Person of Christ

"To the degree that you share in the sufferings of Christ, keep on rejoicing." 1 Peter 4:13

In the town of Stepanvan, Armenia, there lives a women that everyone calls "Palasan's wife." She has her own name, of course, but the people of this small town call her by her husband's name to show her honor. In 1988, a devastating earthquake struck this town in the early noon hour. Mr. Palasan was at work when the quake hit, and he rushed over to the elementary school his son attended. By the time he arrived, the school was already destroyed, but he entered the building to carry children outside to safety. He saved twenty-eight children, but when he went back inside for a final check, an aftershock hit. The school building completely collapsed, and Mr. Palasan was killed.

Being the son of a professional football player was a great honor. To be associated with him when I went to the University of Oklahoma and played basketball (even though his illustrious career there was in football) was also a great honor. Sometimes a person's greatest honor is not who they are but to whom they are related. The highest honor of any believer is to be called a disciple of Jesus Christ, who laid down His life for *all* people. To be called "child of God" is more of an identity and honor than any other name in the universe. The Armenian woman was honored to be called, "Palasan's wife." It is much more of an honor to be called, "a disciple of Christ."

Who do people say that you are? Are you associated with Christ? Do people see you in your lifestyle as a relative of the Creator? Why or why not? How can you obtain that title? Are you willing to do what it takes to get it?

Personal Touch

Sharing Christ

"Let the one who is taught the word share all good things with him who teaches." Galatians 6:6

One of the all-time greatest on the grid iron is a guy named Jerry Rice. He plays for the San Francisco 49er's football team and is considered by most experts the best wide receiver in the history of the NFL. Once, when interviewed, Jerry was asked why he attended such a small, obscure university like Mississippi Valley State University in Itta Bena, Mississippi. Jerry's response was, "Out of all the big-time schools (like UCLA) that recruited me, MVSU was the only school to come to my house for a personal visit." The big-time powerhouse universities send out generic letters, cards, and advertisements, but only this one *showed* Rice personal attention and sincere concern.

When I heard this story it brought to mind just how important personal outreach is. Here is a guy who few thought valuable enough to recruit personally, but now he's a superstar in the sports world. Gang, people, no matter what color or size or nationality, are valuable. How much more important is the personal touch in matters concerning the heart, soul, and spirit of a person. If you're in the business market and you don't extend a personal touch to your clients, then get ready to go belly-up (broke). Wal-mart would not be the nation's number one discount center without friendly smiles, warm handshakes, (low prices) and personal demeanor. Every Wal-mart store in America has a greeter at the door to offer you their services. Christians need to learn from old "Wally World" and make evangelism personal and more practical. Each person you meet deserves your personal best, not your bulk mail worst. Do God, and yourself, a favor and put personal touch into your outreach formula.

Are you giving your *best?* Do you have a tendency to be generic instead of personal in sharing with others? How valuable do you see those who are different from you?

Satan

"Don't be easily deceived brother." James 1:16

The January 1992 issue of *Fortune* magazine featured a piece on "the biggest goofs of 1991." In an act of corporate cooperation, AT&T reached an agreement with the power company of New York City. The contract stated that whenever power demands exceeded the utility's grid, AT&T would lessen their demands by throwing a switch, unplugging some of its facilities, and drawing power from internal generators at its 33 Thomas Street station in lower Manhattan. On September 17th, AT&T acted in accordance with the agreement, but when their own generators kicked in, the power surge knocked out some vital rectifiers, which handled 4.5 million interstate calls, 470,000 international calls, 1,174 flights carrying 85,000 passengers, and total communications systems linking air traffic controllers at LaGuardia, Kennedy, and Newark airports. Alarm bells at the 33 Thomas Street station rang wildly for six hours. AT&T personnel in charge of the rectifiers were away attending a one-day seminar on how to handle emergencies.

What a hilarious story about how we can appear to be prepared on the outside, but remain wide open for an attack. You must be wise to the ways of the wicked or you could be caught in a trap that won't let go without first inflicting much pain to your body and soul. Now, I'm definitely not suggesting that you studying up on all that Satanic stuff, but I am telling you to know he does lurk in the darkness and he will bite you when you least expect it. Prepare yourself for the worst attacks. Be informed what scripture says about Satan so that when an emergency hits, you'll react in the right manner.

How alert are you to Satan's ways? Are you alert to his deceitful schemes? What can you do to be more watchful?

Confession

"For I confess my iniquity; I am full of anxiety because of my sin." Psalms 38:18

A nation wondered what was going wrong in our world when we read the headlines in 1993. The story broke when British police accused two ten-year-old boys of the brutal, ruthless, murder of a two-year-old (that's right...24 months old) boy named James Bulger. The two murderers pleaded innocent to the charges, but the case went to trial. Police investigators noticed how inconsistent the young defendants' alibis were. The climax, which incidentally was never mentioned in the media coverage, came when the parents of one of the accused boys assured him that they loved him as their son and always would. After the trial and examination which confronted them both with irrefutable evidence linking them to the crime, a confession was made. With guilt written all over their faces, the one boy whose parents assured him of their agape love (unconditional) confessed with a soft voice, "I killed James."

I don't believe for one minute that the parents of this young man consented to his actions (murder), yet their love for him was consistent. This is the miracle of God's love. He knows how evil we are, yet He still loves us (you). Confession means that we can admit our worst, horrible sins to Him and be confident that His love for us will never diminish or weaken. Confession is nothing more than "getting right" with our Savior so we can continue in our love relationship. Granted, there is always a consequence for our deeds, just like there was for the young men in this story, yet we can be purified in our hearts. Take a minute to reveal and admit your wrong doing and get right...God will sentence you to freedom, not death. Your sentence was paid two thousand years ago.

When did you last confess your sins to God? Why should you confess daily? Do you think God will forgive you? Will you forgive yourself?

A Facade

Becoming a Christian

"Even so consider yourselves to be dead to sin, but alive to God in Christ Jesus." Romans 6:11

The Washington Post reported a story on October 27, 1993 concerning an elderly woman named Adele Gaboury. When Adele turned up missing, concerned neighbors in Worchester, Massachusetts, informed the police. A brother told the police that Adele had left to live in a nearby nursing home. Satisfied with the information, the neighbors began keeping an eye on the house and watching out for her property. Michael Crowley noticed the mail piling up in the mailbox and decided to deliver it just inside the front door of her home. Adele's next door neighbor began paying ten dollars a week for her grandson to mow and manage the lawn. At one point the grandson believed the pipes had burst in the house because water was flooding out under the front door. He called the utility company to come shut off the water and repair the leak. What no one knew until then was that Adele was inside the house, dead in her bed. Investigation revealed she had died from natural causes *four* years prior.

You see, the respectable appearance of Mrs. Gaboury's house hid the harsh reality inside. Something similar can happen to people we rub shoulders with regularly. They may appear to have it "all together" on the exterior, but their interior is dead. All kinds of religious activities may be happening on the outside while the real problem is missed. They can say all the right things, do all the right deeds, and even put up a front of being "all together," yet no Savior lives inside their heart. Investigate yourself and see where you fall into this story...check out your friends and see if they are dead or alive in Christ. We need life (Christ), not a tidy facade!

Where are you today? Are you alive in Jesus or dead to the world? Do you put on a facade for others just to play the Christian game or has true transformation come through a personal relationship with Christ? How about your friends?

Christ

"No one can serve two masters, either he will hate the one and love the other." Matthew 6:24

It was a spot specifically designated for voicing opinions on any subject matter. Hundreds of people gathered at "Speaker's Corner" in Hyde Park, London, England on a sunny Sunday morning. Talk about a melting pot of humanity! I'm not sure everyone was there for the same reason. Some just happened to drop by, seeing the crowd gathered, but others came to seek out answers to life's questions. Whatever the reason, the intent was obviously to persuade the audience from theory to fact. I was surprised that the subject *all* (not just some) the participants chose to speak on was religion. I mean, come on, freedom of speech to the maximum, and all these milk-crate lecturers chose religion as the topic. The speakers might have selected politics, feminine rights, minority rights, abortion, the death penalty, or any other sizzling topic, but they chose religion...why?

While I was there, five different speakers discussed New Age, Muslim, Hindu, Mormon, and Christianity. I am proud to report the Christian was right-on and the others were one sandwich short of a full picnic. The crowd gravitated to the speaker teaching the truth (which is all bogus and relative without Christ). You see, the "truth" is a *person* (*the truth shall set you free*), not just something you say to stay out of trouble. Everyday we pass those who worship a dead, dull, deceiving god that will get them nowhere. Lesser gods are those gods society follows that offer a *false* sense of security and happiness. Jesus is, and always will be, the *only* God that will be standing when all else falls. Don't be easily deceived, brothers and sisters; don't bite a hook that will get you nowhere but in the frying pan. It is ultimately your choice...just make sure it's the right choice, okay?

What sets Christianity apart from other religions? Why do people historically choose to stay on a religious topic? Are you sure who you worship and believe?

NOW YOU SEE IT, NOW YOU DON'T

Death

"You do not know what tomorrow has in store...your life is but a vapor." James 4:14

It would have been considered a normal day at the office. At 9:03 a.m. on April 19, 1995 federal employees were doing what needed doing in downtown Oklahoma City at the Alfred P. Murrah Federal Building. At 9:04 a.m. the blast from a twenty-four foot Ryder rental truck filled with explosives sent a shock wave, causing total destruction at the site and severe damage to buildings blocks away. Hundreds of fatalities and injuries resulted from the blast consisting of two tons of ammonium nitrate fertilizer, doused in fuel oil, ignited by some sort of detonator. This terrorist act was the worst in US history and stunned the American public. Who and why? Timothy James McVeigh, a twenty-seven year old man portrayed by some in the media as easygoing and introspective, certainly did not seem to fit the profile of someone who could cause this terror. Since returning from the Gulf war though, he reportedly fathered an illegitimate child, lost jobs, drank a lot, fought often, set off explosives, bought guns, occasionally attended right-wing militia group meetings, and lived like a nomad. Timothy was angry at the world (especially the government) for the way the cult compound in Waco, Texas, was handled. He harbored vengeance, fueled by an anger without regard for life, just as long as his statement was made.

Four days after this morning of terror, I was in Oklahoma City for a speaking engagement. I rented a car and was compelled to drive downtown to see the devastation. I stood by the roped off building, wept, and prayed for the victims and their families. I thought about the one minute (9:03) prior to the blast and one minute after (9:05). One minute alive...the next dead. I recalled the verse in James that illustrated to me that our life is a mist...the wisp of steam that rises off an early morning cup of coffee, then vanishes. Life is short and unpredictable. My prayer was that they all (children, men, and women) went to heaven...Amen.

What is anger? How is it manifested? How do you control it? What happens if it's not dealt with?

Walking in the Spirit

"The Spirit himself testifies with our spirit that we are God's children." Romans 8:16

In September 1993, near the close of Major League baseball season, the first-place Philadelphia Phillies were visiting the second-place Montreal Expos. In the first game of the series, the home team Expos came to bat one inning, trailing by a score of 7-4. Their first two batters reached base. The manager sent in a pinch hitter to the plate, rookie Curtis Pride, who had *never* gotten a hit in the major leagues. Pride warmed up, stepped up to the plate, and on the very first pitch laced a double, scoring the two runners on base. The stadium thundered as 45,757 fans screamed and cheered. The Expos third base coach called time out, walked over to Pride, and told him to take off his helmet. "What's wrong with my helmet?" wondered the rookie. Suddenly understanding, he tipped his cap to the fans. After the game, someone asked Pride if he could hear the cheers of the crowd. This person asking the question wasn't giving him a hard time...Curtis is 95% deaf. "Here," Pride said, pointing to his heart, "I could hear it here!"

Sometimes we hear things from God most strongly in our hearts. Just like Curtis Pride heard the approval of the fans, not with his ears, but down deep in his heart. It's in our own hearts that the Creator of the Universe wants us to know His approval of our faith in Christ. To walk in the spirit of Christ means to be so "in tune" with Him that we sense His urgings in our hearts. Think about it...our source of life is not in our minds, or ears, but in our blood-pumping hearts. The ears of our heart become deaf when sin is allowed to deafen them. Sin is a hardening agent that turns our soft, pliable, moldable hearts into granite. Realize that God is the fan who jumps, screams, yells, applauds, and whistles every time we step up to bat against this world and score a victory for His Kingdom.

Where does God speak to you? How soft is your heart? What deafens the ears to your heart? What does it mean to you to hear God's voice?

WARTS

Trials

"To keep me from exalting myself, there was given me a thorn in the flesh, a messenger of Satan to buffet me—to keep me from exalting myself!" 2 Corinthians 12:7

Today we are going to talk about "warts." A wart is something in your life that you wish you didn't have—hair, weight, voice, height, toes, birth defect, mole, physical handicap. If you have ever said, "If I could only get this or get rid of that, it would make my life a lot more enjoyable," then that's a wart. A wart could be petty or small, then again, it could be serious and overwhelming. Take a moment (put this devo on pause) and think about your own warts. A lot of times we try to plead our case with God and explain to Him that if only this wart in our life was gone then everything would be real peachy. Warts make us feel inadequate in life, so we do our best to have them removed or "fixed." Catch this...God's grace is what is adequate, *not* our abilities. Scripture tells us that when we are weak (wart infested), then we are strong in the Lord. In other words, God shines brightest when we (self) are out of the picture. Apostle Paul had a major wart given to him. He didn't do anything to get it (warts are funny that way). The wart definitely kept him from exalting himself; he pleaded with God three times to take it from him. Some folks out there are saying that if you really love God, He will take away all the pain (warts) you have in your life, then everything will be okay. Wrong, amigo. I don't know what Bible they're reading, but it's not like mine. Life is going to be tough and you will have warts. Why? To get rid of self. Warts don't make you ugly like a wicked old witch on Halloween...they make you a dependent child of God.

What warts do you have that hinder you? Would these warts cause you to depend on self or God? What are your warts?

Humility

"Let the brother in humble circumstances glory in his high position." James 1:9

He goes by the show name, "Neon Deon," but his professional name is Deon Sanders. Deon began his quest for stardom at Florida State University as a letterman in two sports, football and baseball. He had incredible speed, quickness, great hands, and an attitude to top it off. He adorned himself in public with gold chains, flashy cars, and dark sunglasses. He was a high draft choice in both the NFL and Major League Baseball upon his final year at FSU. He played for both the Atlanta Falcons football team and the Atlanta Braves baseball team and did well in both. After his second year in the pro's he snatched up another nickname that fits him perfectly, "Prime Time." Why? Because Deon is show all the way when he is performing on the athletic field. Whether it's stealing a base with blazing speed or intercepting a pass and returning it for a touchdown and performing the "shuffle" in the end zone with the world as his audience. "Prime Time" is his name—sports is his fame.

Ironically, while by today's standards all the flash, glitter and gold are "in," Jesus tells us that humility and quiet lives will ultimately deliver the goods. Come on Dodd! Do you think for one minute *that* lifestyle is beneficial? Yep! I do! (I'm kinda' having a conversation with myself.) God's way may not seem to be the most fun and glamorous up front, but I believe it's always the best way. You can almost guarantee that if you observe the world's ways and then do the direct opposite...you'll be pretty close to going God's way. Eternal "Prime-Timers" are the ones who don't bring glory and honor to themselves, but to God. Kinda' showin' God off...now that's showy!

What comes to your mind when you think of humble circumstance? Who is the most humble person you know? Who is the cockiest person you know? Who is honored by their styles? Was Jesus humble or flashy? What humbles you? That's good!

"Do this in remembrance of me." Luke 22:19

You probably remember where this passage of scripture is taken from—the Last Supper. As I was checking this out recently, a thought hit me. Why did Jesus ask His disciples to remember Him while they ate of bread and drank of wine? Was it so that they wouldn't forget Him? Realize His suffering? Give Him the glory? My personal belief on this is simple...when you've got Jesus on your mind, it's hard to sin. I don't know if you practice the cleansing ritual of communion on a regular basis, but I encourage you to do so *at least* once a month. Why? So that you can re-focus your thought-life and your purpose on this planet on Christ. Remembering Jesus turns your eyes off self and on the Savior. The common thread woven in and out of our sin nature is selfishness of our flesh and desires. We can steer clear of a lot of pitfalls and potholes if we only retain our perspective of who Christ is and what He went through on the cross for us. Think on this for a moment...how could you participate in sexual immorality (premarital sex) if Jesus was in the forefront of your mind? How can we (males) lust if all we remember is Christ's love for us?

Our biggest problem as followers of Christ is that we get amnesia and *forget* who we are (disciples) and who Christ is (our Savior from hell). Forgetfulness is a decision, not a sickness or a disease. Train your mind to "dwell" on Christ throughout each and every day you breathe. Learn what peace is obtained by walking in the spirit of Christ in the midst of your chaotic life. Remember, remember, remember where you came from!

How often throughout your day do you remember what Jesus did for you on the cross? Are you a forgetful Christian? What can you do to remember Jesus through a day? When was the last time you took communion?

Working Together

"The whole body, being fitted and held together by that which every joint supplies, according to the proper working of each individual part, causes growth of the body for building up of itself in love." Ephesians 4:16

Margaret and Ruth were an elderly pair living in a convalescent center (old folks' home). They were there due to similar illnesses...they'd both had a stroke. The ironic thing about these two is that Ruth's stroke left the entire right side of her body paralyzed, while Margaret's stroke left the entire left side restricted. Another similarity was that both of these lovely ladies were accomplished pianists in their day. Since the strokes, they had given up hope of ever playing again. One day the director of the center encouraged Ruth and Margaret to sit down at the piano together and play separate solo pieces, each with her good hand. Not only did they develop a beautiful friendship, but they produced wonderful music. This dynamic team began performing concerts for the center and other rest homes in the community.

What a great picture of how the body of Christ is supposed to work in harmony. We have a tendency in our Christian culture to become so "individualized" that we lose vision of how Christ wants the church and para-church organizations to work with one another. A new youth ministry comes into a community and a lot of times the established ministries don't greet the new kid on the block with open arms and acceptance. A lot of churches compete in the numbers game and compare people not as creations of God, but as a barometer for success. Believe you me...real Christians sitting down, planning, talking, setting goals, and performing together make wonderful music for an audience of disbelievers to see. What one member or organization cannot do alone, perhaps two or more could do together—in harmony.

Do you ever see your church or youth group working in harmony with other churches and youth groups? Do you personally "team up" with other believers to accomplish a goal? What can you do personally to show how followers of Jesus should work together?

UNDER THE SEA

Trials

"He rebuked the wind and the surging waves of the sea and it became perfectly calm." Mark 4:39

My feelings on the subject of scuba diving are pretty simple...if God wanted us to breath underwater He would have given us gills. It was totally against my better judgment to try my hand at this sport, but peer pressure overtook me. I first had to go through the difficult procedure of obtaining a license and certification, which I thought was enough. After graduating from scuba school, I was then permitted in the big pool—the ocean. Open water is a lot more different than a pool or lake. Why? 'Cuz there are animals that don't take kindly to us blowfish humans trespassing on their territory. We paid our fee, loaded the giant scuba boat, and drifted out to sea. We headed out to a reef that was home to all kinds of marine life, including sharks (I'd be happier with "Flipper"). The boat tossed around like the S.S. Minnow and I'd swear the crew included Gilligan and the Skipper. Talk about motion sickness (better known as ocean sickness while at sea). I'd never seen waves twenty feet tall or that rough. That all changed once we strapped on our gear and took the Nestea plunge.

The surface seemed out of control, yet below it was calm, quiet, and peaceful. Amazing...how could it be so bad from one perspective and so peaceful from another? It's a lot like God's perspective. We see the craziness, yet God sees the peace. He controls both sides, but from a human's vantage we think God has left us. The turbulent waters that Jesus and Peter walked on were calm below the surface. No matter how tough life may seem, God keeps it all under control if we only dive into the divine. God never leaves us, we leave Him. God's faithfulness is always just a prayer away. We have not (His peacefulness), because we ask not. Dive in!

How peaceful is your life? How much peace do you have in the midst of turbulent trials? How much do you seek God's peace in the midst of your trials?

Pride

"Pride goes before destruction and a haughty spirit before stumbling." Proverbs 16:18

Jose Cubero, one of Spain's most brilliant matadors said, "Pali, this bull has killed me," before he lost consciousness and died. This spectacular matador was only twenty-one years old and was enjoying an illustrious career as one of Spain's all-time greatest. It was in a 1985 bullfight, in a sold-out arena, that Jose made a tragic mistake. He thrust his sword a final time into an exhausted, delirious bull, which then collapsed to the applause of the crowd. Thinking the struggle was over, Jose turned to the crowd to acknowledge the applause. The bull, however, was not dead, and rose to its feet and lunged a final time at the unsuspecting matador. The bull's horn pierced the matador in the back, puncturing his heart. The final scene, much to the crowd's disbelief, was a bull and bullfighter laying dead on the arena floor.

Pride entered the scene long ago in the Garden of Eden. Pride is when we choose to play god and determine our own selfish ways. Pride in any form is a disease that kills humility. As Christians, we are called to live a quiet, humble, pride-less life. We are shown throughout the life of Christ and His three years of ministry, that pride has no place in the Kingdom. Pride does precede a fall for one striving to live in holiness. Pride consists of arrogance, boastfulness, cockiness, flattery, show, and down-right selfishness. Don't let pride jump up out of it's deceit, and take you down to defeat. Pride can kill a friendship, family, and your faith if *you* don't kill it first. Finish it off in your life once and for all, but never turn your back on it. Olé!

What is your definition of pride? Is your definition of humility the opposite? Are you a possessor of pride in your life?

Thoug…

"We are taking very thought captive to the obedience of Chr…
2 Corinthians 10:5

On top of growing up in Texas, I grew up on a ranch, so I thought I'd seen just about everything. It was the spring of 1971 on Callaway's two thousand acre working cattle ranch. If my memory serves me correctly (which is questionable), I recall about thirty pick-ups, the same number of horse-trailers, and forty some-odd cowboys all geared up, ready to rope them doggies. The cattle herd numbered around two thousand five hundred and our job was to sort 'em, cut 'em, rope 'em, and brand 'em. I did all right, holding my own at the age of twelve, until I smelled the rankest smell I'd ever sniffed...skin burning. Now, I'm no genius, but I knew it wasn't some truck seat on fire. My dad tried to explain to me that branding cattle was essential to identify each cow by owner. I'll bet my boots that red-hot metal branding iron with "C Bar W" on it hurt like a big dog. Now, for all you compassionate people, we had a vet on site who administered an ointment that helped cut the pain.

Now that I am an adult (another questionable comment), I look back on this episode in my life and the thought hits me that we as Christians should be branded (marked). Now hear me—not physically, but mentally. Brand your brain by taking all your thoughts captive (like ropin' a cow to brand it) in obedience to Christ. Every time we crack the "Good Book," we should walk away with a lasting mental brand. Let God put His mark that identifies you to a specific owner (Christ) on you (remember...He bought you with a price on the cross). Round up your thoughts daily, rope them down, and put your mark of righteousness on them. Go on cowpokes and rope them doggies.

How do you take a thought captive? Why is it important for thoughts to be filtered by God's Word? What thought do you have that need to be branded?

Sin

[illegible] *ted when he is carried away and enticed by his own* [illegible] *4*

[illegible] s a story about Niagra Falls on a spring day a few years [illegible] e from the hard winter months was breaking up and rush[illegible]g down the river and over the falls in huge chunks. A closer look revealed carcasses of dead fish embedded in the frozen chunks of ice. Hoards of gulls rode on these blocks, pecking away to get to the frozen entree (fish). Just about the time the block of ice (and the gull) were about to take a tumble, the bird would fly away and escape death. On one occasion, a particular gull was engrossed in eating the carcass of a fish, enjoying every bite. When the brink of the falls appeared, out went the wings. The bird flapped and struggled and even lifted the ice block out of the water, but it was too late...its claws had frozen into the ice. The size and weight of the ice was too great, and as the block went over the falls so did the bird, plunging to its death.

The finest attractions of the world become deadly when we are overly attached to them. They may take us to our destruction if we can't give them up. Oh, the danger of delay! Our society has a way of offering something attractive in order to misdirect us in our relationship with Christ. Time is definitely of the essence here and we don't know what fall awaits us around the next corner. Whether it's social status, position, appearance, money, power, or relationships, if it takes your focus and energy off the pursuit of holiness, then it's wrong. No matter how well you think you can ride the illusion...you're not strong enough to escape the weight of worldliness.

What does this world offer you that you'd like to sink your claws in? Are you aware of the dangers that lurk ahead?

Gifts

"I will give thanks to Thee, for I am fearfully and wonderfully made; wonderful are Thy works, and my soul knows it well. Psalms 139:14

There is nothing quite like laying on your back, gazing up on a crystal clear night, looking at the stars. On a dark, quiet night sitting alone just looking up in the sky, at first glance, all the stars seem to be identical. But if you look through a telescope you will notice differences in size, color, intensity, shape, and structure. I bet if you were to crack a few of those stars open like an egg, you'd find each one is even composed differently. You can say the same of people. How similar one seems to the other, just like stars, until you look more closely and get to know them. At that point, a special transformation of thinking and perspective occurs and you realize we all are uniquely different. Even a person's own name is a unique characteristic. You soon realize that each person is made up of a variety of hopes, dreams, theories, perspectives, goals, and cherished thoughts. It's the unique differences that allow us to exist separately and yet combine harmoniously like the multiple pieces of a jigsaw puzzle fit together to form a whole.

God has specifically made each of us different, but at the same time He gave us equal opportunity to develop our gifts and talents. Utilize your special God-given gifts as only you can and learn to accept and encourage the talents of the others. Throw away petty jealousy and have the mature attitude that encourages others to be all they were meant to be in Christ. If you can't win the race yourself, make sure the guy that beats you breaks the world record. Be a Barnabus who saw his limits, but saw Paul's exceptional gifts and encouraged him to use them. Plant trees that you'll never sit under...that's a Christian outlook.

List what you think your talents are. Now, how do you utilize these gifts for God? Are you one of those who doesn't see his/her talents, just those of others? Take a minute to ask God to use you and your talents today.

We're Not Just Playin' Army...It's A War

Spiritual Warfare

"For the weapons of our warfare are not of the flesh, but divinely powerful for the destruction of fortresses." 2 Corinthians 10:4

I guess you could classify me as an "outdoor fanatic," but I consider myself one who just loves to be out in the woods. One of my past motivations for getting out in the woods was hunting trips with my father, but now I find myself out there just to get out of chaos and watch animals on their turf. Living in Colorado offers ample opportunity for watching wildlife. It's just a short trip north to Estes Park, where during the "mid-September Elk Bugle," a natural phenomenon takes place. The males (bulls) of the elk herds battle for dominance, going head-to-head, antler-to-antler, for breeding rights with the females (cows). The largest, heftiest, strongest antlered bull with the most endurance will win the battle of the hormones. The defeated bull leaves and the victorious bull licks its wounds and rests up for the next challenger. The lead "herd bull" will lose hundreds of pounds, tons of strength, and suffer many wounds during the breeding season.

The ironic thing about this natural ritual is that the real battle is won during the summer when elk eat continually. The one that consumes the best diet for growing antlers and gaining weight will be the heavyweight champ of the fight in the fall. Those that eat inadequately sport weaker antlers that break in battle and obtain less bulk for the fall confrontations.

Satan will choose a season to attack and the question is whether we prepared for the battle. Much depends on what we are doing *now* before the war begins. Enduring faith, strength, and wisdom for the spiritual wars ahead are best developed before they're needed. We're not just playin' army...there's a war out there. Go get ready!

In this spiritual war, will you walk away victorious or will you fall to defeat? Is this a serious battle? Do you think you're playin' army, or is it a war?

DISARMED

God's Love

"No height, depth or any other created thing shall be able to separate you from the love of God which is in Christ our Lord." Romans 8:39

On Monday, August 9, 1993, a woman burst into the hospital nursery at the USC medical Center in Los Angeles holding a thirty-eight caliber pistol. Sophia Mardress White came gunning for Elizabeth Staten, a nurse accused of stealing her husband. Sophia fired six shots, hitting Elizabeth in the wrist and stomach. Elizabeth fled and Sophia chased her into the hospital's emergency room. There, with blood all over her clothes and a hot pistol in her hand, she was met by another nurse, Joan Black, who did the unthinkable. Joan walked calmly up to the angry, gun-toting woman and hugged her. As they talked, the hospital invader kept her finger on the trigger. Once, she lifted the hand that held the gun as though she would shoot herself, but the nurse calmly pushed it back down, and continued to hold her. At last Sophia broke into tears and gave up the gun. Nurse Black told reporters later, "I saw a sick person and I felt I had to take care of her."

This gal was disarmed by a hug, by understanding, and by compassion. Jesus looks at us as people who are sick and broken inside, in need of care. It is His embrace that disarms us. What an awesome illustration of God's true love and care for our lives and our future. We, as believers, can be a part of the disarming process by being compassionate, gentle, and caring towards a hostile world of broken souls.

How can you apply this illustration to your life? Do you feel the embrace of the Father? Have you ever disarmed a sticky situation with Christ-like love, understanding (not judgment) and compassion?

Worship

"All the earth will worship Him, and will sing praises to thy name." Psalms 66:4

Having kids is the most awesome experience anyone could imagine. I could write an entire book just on the funny events that happen every second of this "child rearing" stuff. One of the toughest things to get used to, besides changing poopie diapers, is having a little person always checking me out. I can be in bed reading a book (which is a little odd for me), and my kids will stand at the foot of the bed staring at me. Obviously, I've become one of the objects of their fascination...it's weird. After months of seeking them out for play-time, now they choose to come to me. I haven't a clue why, but I figured out that they (my kids) like the idea of coming in and looking at me. They never expect anything in return and all I do is return the smile and they're fine.

The word "worship" means to find worth in something. The simple pleasure of looking at the one you love is what we enjoy each time we worship God and bask in his presence. If there is one thing in our spiritual world that many Christians have lost, it's the act of sincere "worship." There is nothing quite like getting with a herd of fellow sheep (Christians) and doin' some down home praise and worship to our Shepherd. The feeling you get when you praise The Almighty for who He is and what He's done for you is incredible. I think that's why Jesus said we are all to be like children in our faith.

What is worship to you? When was the last time you had a meaningful worship experience? When do you worship God? Where?

WASH UP

Salvation

"Wash me and I shall be whiter than snow." Psalms 51:7

In 1818, Ignaz Phillip Semmelweis was born into a world where women died right and left. Even the finest hospitals lost one out of six young mothers to "childbed fever." In those days, a doctor's daily routine began in the autopsy room, dissecting bodies. From there he made his way to the hospital to examine expectant mothers without a thought to washing his hands first. Dr. Semmelweis was the first man in history to associate such examinations with resultant infection and death. His own practice was to wash with a chlorine solution, and after eleven years and the delivery of over eight thousand five hundred babies, he only lost one hundred and eighty-four mothers (one in fifty). He spent the prime of his life lecturing and debating with his colleagues over this subject. He argued that "Puerperal Fever" was caused by decomposed material transferred to an open wound. None of his fellow doctors believed this theory and instead followed the thinking of doctors and mid-wives who had delivered babies for hundreds of years without washing their hands. No outspoken Hungarian was going to change them now! Dr. Semmelweis died insane at the young age of forty-seven, his wash basins thrown away, his colleagues laughing in his face, and the death rattle of thousands of women ringing in his ears.

If you recall, the anguished prayer of King David after falling to sexual sin was, "Wash me!" "Wash" was the outspoken message to a lost world of pagan peasants. "Unless I wash you, you have no part of me," was spoken by the towel-draped Jesus to an energetic Peter. Without being washed clean by the Savior's blood, we all will die from the contamination of sin. For God's sake, wash!

Do you know someone who has not been washed of their sins? Is washing a physical or spiritual ritual? What's the difference? Are you clean? What can you do to get clean?

DISTRACTIONS

Daily Life

"No soldier in active service entangles himself in the affairs of everyday life." 2 Timothy 2:4

The popular story of Robin Hood is the basis for several recent feature films. In one scene in *Robin Hood, Prince of Thieves,* Robin challenged a young man taking aim at an archery target, "Can you shoot amid distractions?" Just before the boy released the arrow, Robin poked his ear with the sharp bristled feathers on the end of an arrow. The act startled the boy and his shot went high by several feet. After the laughter died down, Maid Marion (a beautiful lady) asked Robin, "Can you?" Robin Hood raised his bow and took aim, his eyes focused intently on the bull's eye. Just as he released the arrow, Maid Marion leaned over and blew into his ear. The arrow missed the target, bounced off the tree behind it and almost hit an innocent bystander.

Distractions come in all types, but whether painful or pleasant, the result is *always* the same: We miss God's mark. As devout followers of Christ we must be so deliberate and intense in our focus that neither big nor small distractions detour our purpose. The Apostle Paul conveys a military message to his good buddy Timothy about not using the affairs of daily life as a focal point. He tells him that a real member of the "God Squad" will stick with his marching orders. Missing the mark due to a distraction is embarrassing for you and others who are watching...just ask the man of Sherwood Forest.

What is your biggest distraction in following God? When does it usually happen? Is there a pattern you can steer clear of? How can you keep focused on God better?

Friendship

"What is desirable in a man is his kindness." Proverbs 19:22

Gentleness is a word not often used in circles of conversation these days. I recall a story from April 19, 1992, about former US Senator John Tower of Texas and twenty-two others. The *Chicago Tribune* headline read, "Gear Blamed in Crash That Killed Senator." A stripped gear in the propeller controls of a commuter plane caused the plane to take a nose-dive into the Georgia woods. A specific gear that adjusted the pitch of the left engine's propellers was slowly worn down by an opposing part with a harder titanium coating, the National Transportation Safety Board reported. It acted like a file and over an extended time period, wore down the teeth that controlled the propeller. Once the teeth were sheared off, the mechanism was not able to continue working.

After reading this article, the thought that we can be a hard material that wears other weaker working materials (people) out hit me like a ton of bricks. Like the titanium-coated gear wore away the softer gear engaged to it, so one abrasive, unkind friend can wear away the spirit of another. To be kind to someone else is to have the spirit of God thriving (living actively) in your life. Don't be a titanium person who goes throughout life wearing down others by abrasive words and actions. Gentleness is a great way to attract friends and bond relationships that will last a lifetime. Abrasion kills others and send friends into a nose-dive of despair.

Would anyone describe you as kind? Why not? Are you an abrasive friend that wears down others? How can you practice kindness in your relationship?

Temptation

"Each one is tempted when he is carried away and enticed by his own lust." James 1:14

It has become a tradition in the Dodd household. We load up the tent, grill, sleeping bags, waders, sunscreen, and BB guns, along with the Dodd boys and old Pops. We head down to Ponca, Arkansas, on the banks of the Buffalo River for our annual father and son canoe trip. Along with about fifteen other fathers and sons, we canoe through the Ozark mountains in a line strung out for miles. The river in the late spring can get kinda' hairy in spots. I have learned, as a kayaker, that the key to not swamping (tumping over) a canoe is how you set it up for rough waters. Good canoers always align the canoe in a proper position to avoid getting caught in a situation of helplessness.

On my latest trip, I realized how we, as Christians, can get into a ton of trouble by setting ourselves up for a spill. I've counseled hundreds of folks who have *put themselves* into a situation that guarantees failure, a place where no follower of Christ should be. The verse above gives us incredible insight that often we put ourselves in predicaments that breed (guarantee) sin. The old saying, "an ounce of prevention is worth a pound of cure," is corny, but true. Don't set a trap, then walk into it and wonder what happened. Sin is deceitful, but not undetectable with the spirit of Christ as a helper. Set yourself up for victory, not a major spill that will leave your life in one uncomfortable state...take it from an experienced river rat.

Do you ever set yourself up for failure? How? What preventative measures can you take?

Uphill Battles

Stress

"Anxiety in the heart of a man weighs it down, but a good word makes it glad." Proverbs 12:25

On my way to a speaking engagement in Grand Junction, Colorado, I was driving uphill (or upmountain) along Interstate 70 through the heart of the Rocky Mountains. I came upon a long freight train headed the same direction, but at a slower speed. I noticed the train was being pushed uphill by two giant diesel locomotives that sounded like they were straining at full power. Now I'm from the great country (I mean state) of Texas, so as a flatlander, I wondered if this was how trains and cargo were moved through the mountains. After a few more miles I caught up to the front of the train and there I found five more diesel locomotives *pulling* the train as well—seven engines in all. Where I come from there's never more than three or four engines on any one train.

That incident was a great visual lesson for me. I'd had several rough months and was under a lot of strain. I was feeling tired and about ready to give it all up to go make "hacky-sacks" in the West Andes Mountains or some weird thing like that. I wondered if I could persevere under all this pressure without blowing a fuse along my journey. Then, a divine thought hit me (like a train). When I am pushing a large load of problems and difficulties uphill with all the strength and stamina I can muster, God is in the lead, *pulling* with power far greater than mine. Now, if that thought doesn't get your motors going at full steam ahead and give you hope to overcome difficulties, then I don't know what will.

How do you handle uphill battles? How do you deal with the times you feel life giving up? How can this illustration relate to you in your life?

Wizard Of Oz

Satan

"And the God of peace will soon crush Satan under your feet and the grace of our Lord Jesus will be with you." Romans 16:20

They seem to be household names in all generations. Dorothy, Toto, Scarecrow, Tin Man, Cowardly Lion, and the Wicked Witch are the familiar characters in *The Wizard of Oz,* along with scenes of flying monkeys, dark and mysterious castles, a city of emerald green, bright red slippers, the yellow brick road, and a farmhouse spinning up to heaven. My personal favorite adventure in Oz is the way Dorothy got back to Kansas. The intimidating Wizard first required items scavenged from the Wicked Witch. The gang returned with the items, but the big Oz reneged on the deal and tried to run them off. It looked as if there'd be no brain for the Scarecrow, no courage for the Lion, no heart for the Tin Man, and definitely no plane ticket for Dorothy and Toto...that is, until the little rat-dog went around back and pulled back the curtain to expose a harmless, little, gray-haired man, claiming to be the Wizard of Oz.

Satan, the fierce lion that roams the earth stalking his victims, is in reality a pussycat. Yes, he does have a lot of tricks up his sleeve, but he was defeated once and for all on a hill called Calvary. The crucifixion of Jesus proved Satan's lack of power and exposed him for what he is...a wimp of a wizard. As a Christian, you are capable of disarming this enemy and his ragged brigade of blundering bean-headed demons at any given moment. You have no need to fear the enemy, but you must be wise to his deceiving smoke-screens. No matter your age, size, or years you have been a believer (Toto was a small dog, notice), you can defeat this enemy with a wave of your Christ-like wand. Click your heals together and say, "I am a winner" three times. You *will* eventually go home, not to Kansas, but heaven.

Are you aware of Satan? Are you scared of him? Think about all the power of Christ you have in your life to defeat and expose him.

A Team Player

Working Together

"Make my joy complete by being of the same mind, maintaining the same love, united in spirit, intent on one purpose." Philippians 2:2

The guru who brought Chrysler Motors out of financial mire was Lee Iacocca. He was a miracle worker; he took control of the automobile producer and brought it out of the woods and into the light, as he did for other powerhouse companies like Ford and General Motors. A man in constant pursuit of perfection, he once asked the legendary football coach, Vince Lombardi, what it took to make a winning team. In Iacocca's book he writes the coach's response to his question:

There are a lot of coaches with good ball clubs who know the fundamentals and have plenty of talent and discipline, but still don't win the game. Then you come to the third ingredient: if you're going to play together as a team, you've got to care for one another. You've got to love each other. Each player has to be thinking about the next guy and saying to himself, "If I don't block that man, Paul is going to get his leg broken. I have to do my job well in order that he can do his." The difference between mediocrity and greatness is the feeling that these guys have for each other.

Whether it's on a team, in a church, running a business, or in a family, healthy survival depends on how much you care for each other and work together toward a common goal. Books dealing with self, individuality, and success sell like hotcakes, but they seldom promote caring for teammates. If God intended us to be "loners" He wouldn't have put us all on the same planet. Two strands are always stronger than one, and so is a team that cares for each individual. You'll never see the letter "I" in the word team. A team player cares more about team success than his own glory. Be a team player. When you win, you *all* win. When you lose as an individual, you lose alone.

How well do you work with others? Are you an individual or team player? Do you care for those you're working with whether it be on a team, at work, church, or in your own family? What do you need to do to become more team oriented? Are you willing to sacrifice?

Sting Of Death

Death

"Knowing that Christ, having been raised from the dead, is never to die again, death no longer is master over Him." Romans 6:9

If you've heard this story before, forgive me for stuttering...if you haven't, yippee! This is a neat story about a father and son driving down a country road on their way to the county fair. It was a spring afternoon, so the windows were down and the 50's music rockin.' All of a sudden, a bumblebee flew into the car window. The little boy, who was allergic to bee stings, was scared to death. His father quickly reached out, grabbed the bee, squeezed it in his hand, and then released it. The boy grew frantic as the bee buzzed about him. The father once again reached out his hand, but this time he pointed to his palm. There, stuck in his skin, was the stinger of the bee. "Do you see this? You don't need to be afraid anymore, I've taken the sting for you."

Who knows if this is a true story or not; that's beside the point. The point is this: We needn't fear anymore if Jesus lives inside our hearts. Christ died and rose again to take the sting of death for us. We, as Christians, don't have to be afraid of what we learn from the newspaper or the ten o'clock news. We shouldn't fear the staggering stats on automobile accident fatalities, AIDS, or drive-by shootings, because we shall experience no sting of death. Why? Because God loves us and will always be with us. The sting has been covered by the sympathy of the Savior.

Are you fearful of death? Why? Isn't it cool that we should have no fear? What does perfect (Christ-like) love get rid of? Are you convinced that Satan's stinger has been disarmed by Christ?

Sin

"For the law of the spirit of life in Christ Jesus has set you free from the law of sin and of death." Romans 8:2

On March 5, 1994, a police officer named Lloyd Prescott was teaching the duties of a Salt Lake City police officer to a class of trainees. During a break, officer Prescott stepped into the hallway for a cup of coffee and saw an unknown gunman herding eighteen hostages into the next room. Acting on instinct, he jumped in line (dressed in street clothes) as the nineteenth hostage. When the gunman announced the order in which hostages would be executed, Prescott identified himself as a cop in an attempt to disarm the gunman. A fight broke out between the fugitive and the officer, and the gunman was killed by his own gun. The hostages were unharmed in the brawl and safely set free.

I share this story to draw a parallel from this struggle between law and lawlessness, to that of good and evil. God dressed in street clothes and entered this messed up world to join those held hostage by sin. This act was not the result of a sense of duty, but love for us and our situation of hopelessness. On the cross, Jesus defeated Satan once and for all, setting us free from the power of sin. Now, I'm not saying we won't struggle or have a battle on our hands, but we have hope in holiness. See the victory in a relationship with Him. Don't be a hostage to sin...be an overcomer. Be set free to enjoy a faith of fulfillment.

Are you a hostage being lead to destruction by sin? Wherein does your hope lie? With Jesus? The world? Yourself? What fulfillment can be found in being released to enjoy life with Christ to its fullest?

Racism

"This I command you, that you love one another just as I (Jesus) have loved you." John 15:12

It has the same potential for destruction as any of the terrorist bombings in Beirut, Manhattan, or Oklahoma City. It's a bomb all right, hidden in the heart of a majority of the world's population. If not defused, it could send us all flying from an explosion of domestic violence and inherited anger. This bomb is called racism. The blood-poisoning of ignorance, misinformation, hate, and anger has been passed down from generation to generation. White, black, yellow, or brown—we must forget the past and stop using *that* as fuel for our present beliefs. God put us all on one planet for a reason. Let me inject this vaccine into your thinking. You won't overcome the hate and anger stemming from racism without a strong dose of Jesus in your heart. I direct an inner-city camp called, "The Sky's the Limit," in the five points region ("the Hood") of Denver. Now, in case you haven't noticed...I'm half white, half Indian. It has been a huge education for me to get involved with "the Hood" and the youth who live there. Love *is* the bridge that allows all colors to come together before anger, hate, and revenge take the spot. No matter your background, *you* have the capability to stop the thinking passed down from generations past. Open your heart to Christ's renewing love and educate yourself. Cross cultural friendships can be some of the most rewarding you'll ever make. Serving a minority, feeding the poor and hungry, volunteering your time and labor to a cause is what Christianity is made of. Be a part of the solution, not the problem, and be a catalyst (leader) in putting an end to racism.

Do you think that racism is a problem? Why? Why not? Do you see yourself as a racist? Do you have friends of another color? What can you do to be a part of the solution, not the problem of racism?

False Prophets

"And in their heart they put God to the test by asking according to their own desire." Psalms 78:18

On a cool, tranquil evening in the Georgia hill country, a congregation trickles into the "Church of the Lord Jesus Christ." Old parishioners chat, young couples juggle babies, and children play amid the pews. Cutting through the church-goers, three men stride quickly, carrying small wooden boxes, and place them near the pulpit. The service begins with a warning, "We have serpents up here and there's death in their bite. If the Lord moves you to handle them, obey the Lord." The pastor pulls out a four foot rattlesnake and a few sleek copperheads to wave around his head. The congregation screams, chants, convulses. This nonsense stems from misunderstanding the verse, *"And these signs shall follow them that believe: In my name shall they cast out devils; speak with new tongues; take up serpents, and if they drink any deadly thing, it shall not hurt them." (Mark 16:17-18).* The snake-handlers accept this verse out of context and believe if they have the faith, they won't get bitten. Suffering bites and deadly venom rarely discourage these people. Even though seventy-five to one hundred people *have* died of bites, there are still those who follow this belief.

There are places of worship that allow a fallen person to deceive clear thinking and good judgment. Gang, God *will not* be mocked or put to the test like a new hi-tech gadget. God is to be worshipped and left in a holy place. God is to be feared and respected as Jehovah. There were false prophets in Jesus' time and they are still around today. These false teachers use magic, illusion, lies, deceit, dictated conviction, control, physical force, and even sex to lure in their prey. James warned us not to be easily deceived. Faith in Jesus isn't avoiding a bite from a poisonous snake, it's, *"the assurance of things hoped for and the conviction of things not seen." (Hebrews 11:1)*

How can you avoid falling victim to a false teacher? How can you avoid taking a verse out of context?

Faith

"Unless you become like little children, you won't enter the kingdom of heaven." Matthew 18:3

It's amazing to me as a parent how we think we will handle our kids differently than our parents handled us. We find ourselves reminding our kids: share, play fair, don't hit, pick up after yourself, if you don't have anything nice to say—don't say anything, don't take things that aren't yours, watch for traffic, say you're sorry, stick together and hold hands. Instructions received from our parents are for our best interest. I find myself giving out orders like a general, because I desire my children to steer clear of the hazards of life. I'm not a big rule person, but I have realized that the rules I initiate in my household are motivated by love for my kids, not because I dig laying down the law.

Scripture is full of boundaries and guidelines to heed for our own good. My boys must have faith that their father knows what's best for his kiddos, and desires the best for their well-being. God has the same perspective as human parents, but we need faith in Him as our Creator to understand. God warns us in His word to flee sexual immorality, love our neighbor, be thankful, never steal or lie, live an unstained life, and so on. Why? Because He wants to be a Hitler god? Not! Because He loves to write rules? No way! Because He is crazy in love with us as His own children? You bet! Heed the warning of Jesus Himself. If you don't have that child-like faith (faith that will jump from anywhere, any height, into your Father's arms because you know He won't drop you), you won't inherit a spot in that heavenly hotel. Grow up and be a child. What??

Are you a child of God? Do you obey your Father in heaven? Did you (or do you) obey your parents' standards?

HELP!

Holy Spirit

"But the Helper (noun), the Holy Spirit, whom the Father will send in My name, He will teach you all things, and bring to your remembrance all that I said to you." John 14:26

Help! How many times have you gotten yourself into a predicament and needed a little help? You searched like a stray dog for a bone of relief, aid, improvement, assistance, and a remedy to your distress. There's nothing like being stranded on the road of life and finally flagging down the assistance that leads you out of a bad circumstance. In *Genesis 2:18,* God said, *"It is not good for man to be alone, I will make him a helper suitable for him."* From the beginning of time, God knew that we would need all the help we could get to make it through life on earth.

In the Old Testament, Christians had prophets like Isaiah, Jeremiah, Ezekiel, Daniel, Hosea, and Joel to help them out in times of chaos. In the New Testament, they had Jesus. But now what do we have? The Holy Spirit. The Greek word "paraclete" is an ancient warrior term. Greek soldiers went into battle in pairs so that when the enemy attacked, they could draw together, back-to-back, covering each other's blind side. The battle partner was a "paraclete." God does not send us into a spiritual battle alone (He even sent His disciples out to the mission fields by twos). The Holy Spirit (Helper) is the battle partner who covers our blind side and fights for our well-being in time of war. Today, you have a Helper to come along side in time of distress, to work with you, like a team works, for one purpose—victory, and to bring it home for the "God Squad." What assurance and peace we have in knowing we can call on God, any time, any place. What a team!

What does the word "Helper" mean to you? Do you allow the Holy Spirit to come back-to-back with you to do battle against the dark side? How can you utilize the Helper more in your daily trials?

Word of God

"That they (people of Israel) may see and recognize, and consider and gain insight as well, that the hand of the Lord has done this." Isaiah 41:10

It was the summer of 1970 and I was playing for the Dallas Little League All-Star team under Coach Hayden Fry, now coach of the University of Iowa football team. Coach had a rule that no one could steal a base unless he first gave the sign. This upset me a lot because I felt I knew the pitchers and catchers well enough to tell when I could and couldn't steal. In one game I decided to steal without a sign from Coach (mistake). I got a good jump off the pitcher and easily beat the throw to second base. After I shook the dirt off my uniform, I smiled with delight, feeling proud of myself. After the game, Coach Fry took me aside and explained why he hadn't given me the sign to steal, and why what I did was foolish. The batter behind me was Eddie, the homerun slugger. When I stole second, first base was left open, so the other team walked the slugger intentionally, taking the bat out of his hands. The next batter hadn't been hitting the ball well, so Coach intended to send in a pinch hitter to try and drive in the men (me) on base. That left Coach Fry without bench strength later in the game when he needed it.

The problem was, I saw only my capability to steal. Coach Fry was watching the whole game, not just one inning. We too, see only so far, but God sees the bigger picture. When He sends us a signal, it's wise to obey, no matter how much we may think we know. God is the coach in the game of life because we aren't capable. Listen and obey, it's the only way.

Have you ever done anything on your own call despite warnings from your authority? Did you blow the game for your team, family, friends?

BUILDING CODES

Trials

"Persecuted, but not forsaken, struck down, but not destroyed." 2 Corinthians 4:9

A TV camera crew for the local news was assigned to report on the widespread destruction of Hurricane Andrew in southern Florida. In one scene, amid devastation and debris, only one house stood on its foundation. The owner of the house was cleaning up the yard when a reporter approached. "Sir, why is your house the only one still standing? How did you manage to escape the severe damage of the hurricane?" asked the reporter. "I built this house myself," the man replied. "I also built it according to the Florida state code. When the code called for two by six roof trusses, I used two by six roof trusses. I was told if the house was built according to code it could withstand a hurricane. I did, and it did. I suppose no one else around here followed the code."

You know, when the sun is shining and the skies are blue, building our lives on something other than the guidelines in God's Word can be a temptation. What we must remember in light of pleasant circumstances is that there is a hurricane coming—for everyone. The hurricane will strike suddenly and without warning. It may come in the form of death, persecution, suffering, or trial. The funny thing about hurricanes is that they show absolutely *no* favorites. Trials are a lot like that, you know—no favoritism. Build your life on God's precepts and instruction. God laid out a building code back when codes weren't in style. When a hurricane is about to hit, there is a lot of comfort (not panic) in *knowing* that your life is built on the truth of God.

Name three building codes God spells out in His word for you? When did the last hurricane (trial) hit your home (life)? Were you left standing or devastated? How often do you study God's codes? Daily?

Deeds

"Deeds that are good are quite evident, and those which are otherwise cannot be concealed." 1 Timothy 5:25

Major Osipovich, an air force pilot for the former USSR, planned to give a talk on peace at his children's school. He would need time off, so he volunteered for make-up night duty. That is how he found himself patrolling the skies over eastern regions of Russia on September 1, 1983—the very night a Korean airlines flight accidentally strayed off course into Soviet air space. Osipovich was caught in a series of blunders and mis-communication that night. When all was said and done, he followed his orders from control central in Moscow and shot down an unidentified aircraft. The actions of an air force pilot preparing to talk to a bunch of kids about peace, not only caused two hundred and forty innocent passengers to die, but sparked an international incident that pushed world powers to a military stand-off.

Even though this mishap was unintentional, it exemplifies that even though talk is important, actions carry far more weight. We can learn a valuable lesson. Our deeds are powerful. Innocent spectators watch for the truth of scripture in us. We can totally blow our witness and damage our testimony with one single deed. Now, I'm not saying we must be perfect little angels with spotless lives. I *am* saying we should walk carefully and realize how our actions speak louder than words. Learn to walk your talk. Every time we exemplify sin in our flesh, we not only set ourselves back, but a whole lot of other believers trying to make a significant impact for Christ. What we do, much more than what we say, makes a real impact.

How do people view your deeds and actions as a Christian? What is more important to Christ, what we say or who we are? How can you avoid fatal deeds?

Dream Team

Dreaming

"Where there is no vision, people parish." Proverbs 29:18

You're never too old for a trip to see Mickey and Minnie Mouse. There is no place on this planet, I believe, with more fun rides, atmosphere, or a better theme than Disney World. There's a story that when Walt Disney purchased the cheap swamp land in Orlando, he first held a huge party and invited everyone who would be a part of building the park. Electricians, plumbers, carpenters, welders, bulldozer operators, concrete layers, painters, designers, engineers, and technicians all were included. An architectural firm built a model of the theme parks, and Walt had it displayed at the cook-out so workers could see the dream they were building. His desire was that workers would devote not only their labor to the project, but also their hearts.

Soon after the completion of Disney World, someone said, "Isn't it too bad that Walt Disney didn't live to see this?" Mike Vance, creative director of Disney Studios replied, "He did see it—that's why it's here." People need to dream more and learn to instill their dreams in others. When you stop dreaming, you start dying. Let your uninhibited creative juices flow and dream a little. Catch the vision that God has for you as His child. Dream of a place called heaven where there will be no pain, hate, sorrow, or tears—a place of joy, love, peace, and eternity with your Savior. Be a member of the "Dream Team!"

What is your biggest dream? Do you share your dreams with others? What stops you from sharing your dreams? Take a thirty minute walk alone this week to dream a little.

A Rubber Band

Trials

"For the Lord your God is testing (stretching) you to find out if you love Him with all your heart and with all your soul." Deuteronomy 13:3

Now, you talk about a wacko thought fixin' to fly out of nowhere. Recently, I was performing my morning ritual, which includes reading the morning newspaper at the breakfast table. When I rolled off the rubber band that holds the paper together, it flew up and smacked me in the bottom lip. After my blood pressure subsided, a thought hit me as well. Are you ready for this one? A rubber band is *only* useful if the object it surrounds is bigger than it is. Let me rephrase that...a rubber band is *worthless* if you put it around anything that doesn't stretch it. Catch my drift?

I'm sure that if rubber bands had feelings and could talk, they would tell you they don't much appreciate being stretched, pulled, and twisted to serve someone else's purpose. As Christians, we don't take kindly to being stretched by God in our lives either. You hear all the time how people really want to be stretched and grow in life. Yeah, right. We say that, but in our minds, we want to be stretched our way, on our time table, and painlessly to boot. God doesn't work that way. He has to catch us off guard and do it His way or we really don't get the full perspective or learn the lesson. You see, when we are stretched, we have no one else to lean on except God (and He likes it that way...no other providers). Death, rejection, failure, humiliation, despair, broken hearts, and separation are some means God may use to draw us to Him. I saw a billboard by a church once that read, "Anything that causes you to pray is a good thing." How true that is!

When does God stretch you? How often? Do you ever feel like you're gonna' break? Why does God use the stretching method to teach and mature us as followers? How do you handle being stretched? Can you see the value in it?

Sin

"In order that no advantage be taken of us by Satan; for we are not ignorant of his schemes (disguises)." 2 Corinthians 2:11

One of my favorite friends also happens to be a big animal lover. He has four children who know their father has a soft spot for critters. On one occasion, he caught a baby raccoon and brought it home for the kids to see. At a family dinner meeting that night, they came up with a name for the new arrival—"Bandit." One fact about raccoons they seemed to overlook is that as they mature, these animals go through a glandular change and often become aggressive to the point of attack. Since a thirty-pound raccoon can equal a one hundred pound dog in a fight, they can be the source of extensive hospital bills. I recall talking to the nine-year-old daughter about the dilemma and her response was, "Bandit wouldn't hurt me...he just wouldn't!" But, after several friends of the family and their own kids suffered puncture wounds and face lacerations, they released the beast back to the wilderness.

I'm reminded how sin often comes disguised (dressed) in an adorable appearance, and as we play, it becomes easy to say, "It will be different for me," but the result of this type thinking is predictable. Sin is like fire—if you mess with it, you will get burned. Don't be taken in (lured) by Satan's appearance as a harmless creature, but be wise to his power and schemes to destroy you...the wounds can be fatal!

Are you deceived by sin's disguise? Do you ever think you are superman or superwoman, capable of taking on sin? How can you wise up to sin's game?

Search And Rescue

Salvation

"For the Son of Man has come to seek and to save that which was lost." Luke 19:10

On the night of April 15, 1912, the Titanic sunk to the floor of the Atlantic, some two and a half hours after hitting an iceberg that tore a three hundred foot gash in her starboard side. Although twenty life-boats and rafts were launched, they were too few and only partially filled. Most passengers ended up struggling in the icy seas while those in the life boats waited a safe distance from the sinking vessel. Lifeboat #14 did row back after the "unsinkable" ship slipped from sight to chase cries in the darkness, seeking to save a precious few. No other boat joined #14 for the rescue mission (even though they were only about half full), *fearing* that a swarm of unknown swimmers might flip their safe boat and swamp them in the frigid seas. Members of the rescue mission that eventually found the life-boats never quite understood how fear (selfish fear) could prompt the survivors to *not* help as they watched hundreds die in the violent sea that night.

In His mission statement, Jesus says that He has "come to seek and save," and has commissioned us to do the same. I find that most Christians have good hearts and a willing spirit, but they often go down in defeat to the arch rival, *fear.* While people drown in the treacherous waters around us, we are tempted to stay all safe and dry and make certain no one rocks our security boat. What we don't understand is that the life boats aren't our own, so safety comes only at the expense of the One who overcame His fear with love to save us. Don't let the security and safety of your present position as an heir to the Kingdom, and the fear of rejection, stop you from throwing a life-line to the lost souls bobbing around your daily life. Paddle, boy...paddle!

Do you fear sharing Jesus with someone else? Are you sitting in your nice, safe, cozy world watching and hearing the cries of the drowning victims? Make it your goal to tell a lost person about the love of Jesus today? (Fear later!)

Happy Meal

Happiness

"Happy are the people whose God is the Lord." Psalms 144:15)

I can't help but think about "Mickey D's" when I talk about my kids. The "golden arches" hypnotize the kid population of America to believe the only place to eat is McDonald's. I think my kids learned to say "Happy Meal" before "Mommy" or "Da-da." For years I've tried to understand the lure (magnetism) of those golden arches to the twelve and under population. Marketing strategy is directed at kids, not parents. If I'd bought stock in this billion dollar company years ago, I'd be a rich man about now, due in part to all the money I've spent myself buying Happy Meals. Now, catch this thought with me...what about these Happy Meals? Why do kids desire them so? Is it the food? Is it the free dinky ice cream cone, or the toy surprise? I don't have the answer, but I know that they do what they intend to do—make kids (mine, especially) *happy!*

Adults have a similar diversion, but they call it "happy hour." The purpose is to provide beverage and atmosphere to take the edge off a work day. My question is: Why do we need a specific meal or hour to be happy? Does it mean that for the other twenty-three hours we should be sad? We (Christians) are a chosen people of royal lineage whose sheer existence as children of God should mean happiness. We have a reason, through God's grace, to be joyful and bubble over with excitement at the kingdom that awaits us. Happiness is a frame of mind, an attitude, an awareness, an understanding, a gift. You *don't* need a meal, hour, material gift, cause, promotion, award, mortal relationship, deed, or anything else to be happy. Like the song say, "Don't worry...be happy!" And watch out for Ronald's house...it will steer your car right in.

Are you considered happy by your peers? What makes you happy? Does knowing you're a child of God? Why or Why not? Do you like Big Mac's?

HONEST ABE

Integrity

"My honesty will answer me later." Genesis 30:33

For Coach Stroud of the Rockdale County High School Bulldogs in Conyers, Georgia, it was meant to be a championship basketball season. With twenty-one wins and only five losses they were on the way to the Georgia boys' basketball state tournament. The final game was best of all, with a remarkable come-from-behind victory in the closing moments. The Bulldogs proudly displayed their State Championship trophy in the case outside the gym. Then tragedy struck. The Bulldogs were stripped of their title after school officials learned that a player on the team, who played only forty-five seconds in the first of the school's five post-season games, was found scholastically ineligible. They received this information directly from Coach Stroud. The ineligible team member played only a few seconds all season, but still Coach Stroud confessed. Others told him to just keep quiet and the incident would pass unnoticed, but not in the conscience of a man of honesty and integrity. Coach gathered his team together in the locker room and told them, "People forget scores of games; they don't forget what you're made of."

Integrity and honesty are hard to come by in this world of unfaithfulness and deception. You have to look hard and long to scare up rare men and women of their word. What an awesome (I like that word, if you can't tell by now) example Coach Stroud is to us. There is more to life than winning and losing.

Are you a person of honesty? How would you define integrity? What circumstances come up in your life that cause you to be dishonest? How can you overcome that temptation?

Trials

"You saw with your own eyes the great trials, the miraculous signs and wonders, the mighty hand and outstretched arm, with which the Lord your God brought you out. The Lord your God will do the same to all the peoples you now fear." Deuteronomy 7:19

Watch the weather channel from around the first of July until mid-October, and you'll most likely hear about forest fires in the western United States. In 1994 dozens of fires were set by both careless campers and natural causes, scorching millions of acres and destroying forest land in approximately half of Yellowstone Park. Most folks across the nation saw this as a total disaster. However, former Yellowstone Park Superintendent, Thomas O. Hobbs, said good things come out of seemingly bad situations. He went on to explain that major fires actually benefit the park in the long run. "Burnouts" rejuvenate park land by cleansing it of insect and plant disease before the natural growth cycle starts again.

Let me draw a parallel from this disaster to the devastation in human lives. Trials and tough times come in so many different ways like: death, financial failure, disappointment, and unintended heartache. As we go through trials, we may feel as if we've been dealt a bad hand. We can't imagine a loving God allowing these disasters to happen to us in light of our walk with Christ. The point we miss is that down the road of time, we will see *new* growth and rejuvenation. In the end, we are strengthened with a newfound faith and dependence on God. Remember that God sees *not* as man sees and that He is in total control of every situation, no matter how out-of-control it may seem to us. Try not to start your own fires, but when God starts one, let it do what it's intended to do...clean out the old and bring in the new.

Why is it so important to allow God to clean up our lives with trials? Is this process fun? How should we respond to His fires in life? How can we prepare for a burnout?

Prayer

"I urge then, first of all, that requests, prayers, intercession and thanksgiving be made for everyone." 1 Timothy 2:1

During Operation Desert Storm, the Iraqi war machine (the tank) was overwhelmed by the Coalition Force's ability to strike strategic targets with never-before-seen accuracy. Unknown to the Iraqis, the Allied Supreme Command dropped "Special Operations Force" (SOF) units deep behind enemy lines. These men provided bombing coordinates for military targets and first-hand reports on the effectiveness of subsequent bombing missions by the US Air Force. To avoid unintended targets, pinpoint bombing was often required. A soldier from an SOF unit, standing on the ground, would request an aircraft high overhead to drop a laser guided missile. Using a hand-held laser, the soldier would point at the target. The missile would lock on the target for a direct hit.

In much the same way, the prayers of Christian focus are often general in intent. Our prayers and conversations with God should target specific needs and petitions. A good way to pray is:

1. Praise God for who He is.
2. Confess sins.
3. Petition for needs of others.
4. Thank Him for answers which come as yes, no, or wait.

Take time out of each day to commune with God. Pray specifically for things you would like to see Him take over. Pray to Him like you would reveal needs and concerns with your best friend. Prayer is what we need to do before we do anything. Prayer and God's Word are the only two offensive weapons we have as Christians. Use them wisely and you *will* win this spiritual war.

Spend the next fifteen minutes praying.

DISCHARGED

Trials

"In this you greatly rejoice, though now for a little while you may have had to suffer grief in all kinds of trials." 1 Peter 1:6

I'm slowly figuring out this family stuff. I'll do my best to try and share a few helpful hints so that your learning curve will be less dramatic. First and foremost, when you find out you're "expecting," purchase a video camcorder. There are about two thousand different types of camcorders on the market, old fashioned, big ones, palm size, or picture view. Costs range from hundreds to thousands, depending on your weakness for gimmicks (bells and whistles), or your preference for quality. You can buy all sorts of junk with them like bags, tripods, and lenses. Whatever you buy, you'd best get several batteries and lots of video tape.

After I purchased my camcorder, I then read the instructions (which is uncommon for me) on the use of the battery. The manufacturer recommend that the battery should completely discharge before recharging it, especially the first few times. This procedure actually increases the endurance of the battery.

In a like manner, our trials in life "discharge" us, emptying our dependence on self (our own human strength) and increasing our capacity to receive God's limitless power to endure. It's not easy to totally eliminate self and allow God to intervene as our true power source. To "discharge" means to acknowledge that *we* are incapable, yet our Savior is very capable. Trials are in our path to teach us endurance, to mature us, and to deepen our faith and love for God. Next time you're playing with one of those one-eyed monsters and the battery runs out, recall that the same will happen to you someday. Recharge it to full power...Jesus will recharge you.

How do you handle the times when you are completely depleted of self? How do you recharge yourself? Is God anywhere in the picture? Why does God allow trials to discharge you?

Don't Give Up

Running the Race

"Do you not know that those who run the race all *run, but only the one receives the prize? Run in such a way that you may win." 1 Corinthians 9:24*

Mamo Walde of Ethiopia finished first in the twenty-six mile marathon at the Mexico City Olympic Stadium on October 29, 1968. An hour and a half later, the last of the marathon runners were carried off to the first-aid station, exhausted. As the remaining spectators prepared to exit the stadium, those near the gates heard the sound of sirens and police whistles. Everyone turned to look as a lone figure, wearing the colors of Tanzania, entered the darkened stadium. His name was John Stephen Akhwari and he was the last participant to finish the race. He entered the stadium on legs all bloody and bandaged, severely injured in a fall, and he grimaced with each step. The remaining spectators rose and applauded him as if he were the winner. After crossing the finish line, Akhwari slowly walked off the field without turning to the cheering crowd. Seeing how he was injured and had no chance at all of winning the race, a reporter asked this young man why he didn't just quit and get medical attention immediately. The runner replied, "My country didn't send me seven thousand miles to start the race, they sent me seven thousand miles to finish it."

You just don't find many folks these days with a focused, die-hard attitude in whatever they do, whether it's sticking with a job, playing sports, remaining married, staying consistent in their walk with Christ, or whatever. I call those who stick with it, "people with a purpose." Our society is training up and cheering on a quitter's mentality of "when the going gets tough, quit," instead of "when the going gets tough, the tough get going." Realize that every time you start something and don't see it to completion, you're developing a life-long pattern. Start now to live by the motto, "Quitters never win and winners never quit."

Why is it so hard to stick with it? Have you ever started something and not finished it? Why? How can you develop a die-hard attitude?

JUST BE

Hearing God

"Be still and know that I am God." Psalms 46:10

Before refrigerators and ice boxes, people used to use windowless ice houses with thick walls and a tightly fitted door to store food. In the winter, when streams and lakes were frozen solid, large blocks of ice were cut and hauled back to the ice houses, stacked, and covered with sawdust. Most of the time the ice lasted well into summer. Once, a man lost a valuable watch while working in an icehouse. He searched for days, but to no avail. His fellow workers and neighbors looked for the watch, but came up short. A young boy heard the rumor of the lost watch and slipped into the ice house unnoticed one day and walked out an hour later with the valuable watch in his hand. Amazed by the boy's find, the others asked how he did it. He replied, "I walked in, laid down in the sawdust, and listened for the ticking of the watch."

"Being still" is definitely not a common practice in society today. Appointments, meetings, deadlines, and day-timers seem to crowd out any hope of finding peace in our daily routine. Often, the question is not if God is speaking to us (in our hearts, not verbally), but whether we are ever still enough to hear Him. No one gets a lot of praise or pats on the back for being still. We are a nation of doers, not sitters, but when we try to seek counsel and guidance from God in the midst of our daily rush, the world's noise overcomes His urgings. Find time each day to sneak off in a quiet corner of your house, office, school, or whatever, to be with, and in the presence of God. The reward will be far more valuable than any lost watch, I can guarantee that.

When was the last time you were "still" with God? Did you know communication consists of both talking *and* listening? What gets in the way of finding quiet time? Where could you go to be still?

Sin

"The sting of sin is death." 1 Corinthians 15:56

One of my favorite childhood memories was spending time with my Dad on our ranch in Decatur, Texas. He trained horses for racing, so as you might imagine, the work was hard and the days were long. My recreation was hunting bullfrogs on a tank (in Texas that's what we call a pond) with a twenty-two caliber rifle. One day I was walking along the shore looking for those beady eyes and saw a small, green, tree frog half-way in the water's edge. He didn't jump as I got closer and I noticed how dumbstruck and dull his eyes were. As I watched, he slowly began to deflate and sag. His skin emptied and drooped, and even his little skull began to collapse like a falling tent. The frog sank as an oily fluid circled his body. I remembered reading about a water bug, an enormous brown beetle that eats tadpoles, insects, and frogs. Its legs grip and hook inward as it seizes its victim and paralyzes it with enzymes. It only takes one bite to release a poison that literally dissolves the prey's muscles, bones, and organs (all but the skin). It sucks out the victim's body, reducing it to a juice (gross, isn't it?).

Sin is like this giant water bug in that hidden sin paralyzes our inner spirit and constricts our heart. It can suck the joy right out of us and leave us dead in the water. Sin is weird that way, it shows no favorites and attacks without mercy. Only God can rescue us from sin's deadly grip through confession and sincere repentance. Even though this story puts an unsettling pit in the stomach, it is not nearly as repulsive as a believer shrinking down to nothing. Don't swim in waters (circumstances) that tend to nurture giant water beetles (deceptive sin) as permanent inhabitants. Be aware!

Has sin ever gotten a grip on you? Did it begin to suck the life and hope right out of you? What do you do about such a vicious killer? How can you avoid getting caught in its grip?

Faith

"The righteous man shall live by faith." Romans 1:17

On the news a few years back, I saw a photographer who would skydive in order to take incredible photos of guys jumping from planes, ten thousand feet up. His photos appeared in magazines like *National Geographic, Outside,* and *Aviation.* On this day, the photographer jumped with a group to take shots of their decent and aerial stunts. He took photos all the way down, even as his companions opened their parachutes. As the final skydiver opened his chute, the picture went berserk. The announcer reported that the cameraman had fallen to his death, having jumped out of the plane, accidentally wearing *no* parachute. It wasn't until he reached for the ripcord that he realized he was free-falling without a 'chute. Tragically, he had acted thoughtlessly and with haste. Nothing in this world could have saved him, because his faith was in a parachute he never buckled on.

You know, faith is a funny thing. It's not limited to the Christian vocabulary, either. People have faith in worldly things like money, relationships, insurance, and careers. They may have faith in the wrong god or the wrong leader. Faith in anything but an all-sufficient God can be just as tragic, spiritually. Only with faith in Christ do we dare to step into this dangerous life. Make sure, if you're betting all your chips (your life) on one roll of the dice, that you bet on Christ and not an insecure worldly system. Faith is only faith if you have it resting on the supreme Savior. Look before you leap...but after seeing it's Christ, then jump. The ride will be exciting and the landing guaranteed.

In what do you have faith as you jump in the game of life? In what does the world tell you to put your faith? How can you avoid false faith so that when you reach for the ripcord of righteousness, it's there?

Worldliness

"Since you died with Christ to the basic principles of this world, why, as though you still belonged to it, do you submit to its rules." Colossians 2:20

To be defined means to be calculated and prescribed for a stated meaning or purpose. I've never been one to spend free time reading the dictionary, but this thick book contains the meaning of every word in the English language. Even if you never knew a word existed, you'll find it in good old Webster's.

Our society defines thoughts, beliefs, theories, and standards through the avenues of music, radio, television, newspapers, and magazines. Billions of dollars are made each year by exploiting viewers and readers. These media vessels have also clued in that they can teach and mold a generation's way of thinking. What was considered vulgar and pornographic thirty years ago is now acceptable. Sex, violence, homosexuality, abortion, extra marital activity, and a long list of other things can be seen on prime time TV, or in million-subscriber magazines. Best selling books and albums (music) are at the top, not because of their brilliance, but corrupt content. Why? Because we have been trained to listen to, read, and watch things that are appealing to our flesh. Pigs love to wallow in the mud and so does a culture living in sin. We must *stop* defining ourselves and let God, through His Word, remold and re-program our way of thinking. These worldly vessels (media) should be down-right offensive to our spirits and repulsive to our minds. Stop it! Stop letting some guru at the controls of TV, record labels, publishing, and so on, define your convictions. Take an active stand against such evils and boycott what's not right. Don't go to bad movies, don't buy CD's that have negative lyrics, don't buy pornographic publications, don't subscribe to liberal newspapers. No, you won't put them out of business, but you *will not* help fund their efforts, and that *is* doing something about it.

Do you feel you are exploited by the media in any way? Are your thoughts, beliefs, and standards being defined by them? What should be defining you? How can you be redefined?

Guilt By Association

Discipleship

"Now Peter was standing and warming himself. They said to him 'You are not also one of His (Jesus) disciples, are you?' and he denied it and said, 'I am not.'" John 18:25

Good old Peter is back in the headlines for this devo. I think I enjoy learning more about the Apostle Peter than any one of the other disciples because he reminds me of me. You could call him, "Mr. Peppermint Socks," because he always has his foot in his mouth. At the time of this event, Judas betrayed Jesus for fifty bucks and Jesus was brought before Annas, the priest of that year. Jesus was questioned by the high priest and an officer gave him a shot in the ribs (sucker punch) for His supposedly poor presentation. A slave girl saw Peter standing around the fire with some guards at the temple and asked him if he wasn't one of those associated with this Jesus. Peter, wanting to protect himself, quickly shunned the comment. After the cock crowed, after his third denial, Peter recalled Jesus' prophecy (prediction). Jesus went before Pilate, ultimately to the crucifixion.

I don't imagine Peter (a loyal follower) planned to deny ever knowing Jesus. I think Peter had a great heart of courage, but at that moment, things were getting heated. Guilt by association still happens today if your lifestyle reflects a relationship with Christ. An association is a group of people with a common goal, purpose, or belief. In our world we have all sorts of associations barking out their beliefs and surrendering to the group cause. What an honor it is to be found guilty of following Christ. If you're ever gonna' be found guilty of anything, make sure it's of following Jesus too closely.

With what would your friends consider you to be associated? Have you ever been associated and found guilty of being a Christian? Why or why not?

Dreams

"Older men will dream dreams and your young men will see visions."
Joel 2:28

Auguste Bartholdi traveled from France to Egypt in 1856. There, the grandeur of the pyramids, the Nile, and the beauty of the stately desert Sphinx aroused his artistic mind. In Egypt, he met Ferdinand de Lesseps, who was there to sell the idea of digging a canal from the Red Sea to the Mediterranean, so merchant ships would no longer have to travel around the tip of Africa. Ferdinand's concept inspired the artist Auguste to design a lighthouse for the entrance of the canal. This lighthouse wouldn't be an ordinary one, it would symbolize the light of western civilization flowing to the East. It took over ten years to build the Suez Canal, so Auguste had time to design and build many clay models. He scrapped plan after plan until he found the right figure, the perfect design. Only one problem remained...who would pay for it? He searched everywhere, but no one was interested in his idea. The Suez Canal opened, but without a lighthouse. Defeated and discouraged, Auguste returned to France, ten years of work wasted. His lighthouse would have been a colossal robed lady standing taller than a pyramid. She would hold the book of justice in one hand and in the other, a torch that would guide merchant ships to the canal. Back in France, the French Government sought a gift for America. They chose Auguste's lighthouse, which today stands in the New York harbor and is called the Statue of Liberty.

This is a wonderful account of how great dreams eventually find the right door. Who knows, maybe one of *your* dreams could become a reality if you just stick with it. It amazes me how God can use the ideas of His people and orchestrate a reality. You have all the ability and talent to pull off such a stunt, if you give your ideas and dreams to Him in prayers of petition.

Do you have a dream that few know? What are you doing to help those ideas become real? Have you told God through prayer about those dreams? Why not? Go do it!

Christian Race

"Fixing our eyes on Christ, the author and perfector of our faith." Hebrews 12:2

Eamon Coghlan was the Irish world record holder at fifteen hundred meters and was running in a qualifying heat at the World Indoor Track and Field Championships in Indianapolis, Indiana. With two and a half laps left in the race, he was accidentally tripped and fell to the track surface. Eamon didn't get to be a record holder by having a quitter's attitude, so he pulled himself up to his feet, and with incredible effort, managed to catch up to the leaders in the race. With approximately twenty yards left to the finish line, he was in third place—good enough to qualify for the finals. Eamon looked over his left shoulder and saw no one even close to him, so he let up to coast the last ten yards. What he hadn't seen was a runner charging up over his right shoulder with the momentum to pass him at the finish line, thus eliminating him from the finals. His great comeback after a fall was rendered worthless by taking his eyes and heart off the finish line.

In today's world of chaos and fast lanes, it's tempting to let up when it looks like things around us are favorable. We feel comfortable the way we are and the way life is going for us, so we coast. We take it out of four wheel drive and put it in neutral. The problem comes when our wheels begin to slip, we lose our momentum, and risk losing the race. I have always admired those few individuals that finish the race as excited and determined as when they started. Be the runner on God's track team that stays focused on the goal, purpose, and reason (Jesus). You may get tripped up during this race, so have the mind-set going into it that you *will not* quit and you *will* get up. Make a set-back be a comeback.

What conditions cause you to take your eyes off Christ? When are you tempted to just coast instead of press on? How can you become the type of Christian that finishes as strong as they start?

Sin

"Who can discern his errors? Acquit me of hidden faults. Keep back your servant from presumptuous sins." Psalms 19:12-13

There is no place on this planet like the Rocky Mountains. I participated in a hiking expedition atop a fourteen thousand foot peak, looking out over God's vast creation of wilderness. Being the picture freak that I am, I noticed off to the west, a large mass of dark clouds moving in our direction. I could see the last glimpse of sunlight peaking over the thunderstorm and a brilliant lightning display below. I decided to take a few photos of this spaghetti-like web of lightning bolts. You should have seen (and you still can if you want a picture) this fireworks show God put on for us.

I realized how, in much the same way, our sins present themselves before the eyes of our Lord. Where we see only *one* isolated or individual act, God sees the overall web of our sin. To us, what seems insignificant and passes without notice, creates a dramatic display from God's panoramic viewpoint. God sits at a perspective (vantage point) that you and I as fallen people can't see. God is no doubt a forgiving Creator, in the business of forgetting our sins. Problems arise when we don't even know we are in the wrong. Wouldn't it be great if God could fax us those sins we think are too insignificant to cause a tiff about? He does...by the Holy Spirit. We shouldn't play the comparison game with other believers or society to gauge how well we are doing. We must use scripture as our basis and barometer. There is "freedom" with Christ, but there is also a hint of fear. Be careful not to grade your own papers to determine your overall performance in God's classroom. Let the Bible govern the correct answers and compare your test with the Master's copy.

What sin keeps coming back to haunt you? Do you ask the Holy Spirit to reveal those hidden sins? Why not?

Rescue 911

Salvation

"That if you confess with your mouth, 'Jesus is Lord,' and believe in your heart that God raised him from the dead, you will be saved." Romans 10:9

The Reader's Digest reported the incredible story of Walter Wyatt's flight from Nassau to Miami (normally a one hour flight) on a stormy night in December of 1986. Thieves had broken into his private twin-engine plane to steal valuable navigational instruments. With only a compass and a hand-held radio, Walter flew into skies blackened by storms. When his compass gyrated, he knew he was going the wrong direction. He put out a "May Day" for the Coast Guard Falcon search plane. But at 8 p.m., he ran out of fuel and could do nothing but crash-land in open water. Walter survived the crash, but the plane sank quickly, leaving him floating alone in the rough waters. With blood on his forehead, he floated on his back until he felt a hard bump on his back—a shark. He floated ten hours until morning when he saw the dorsal fin of another shark headed for him. Twisting, he felt the hide of a shark brush against him. In a moment, he was surrounded by dozens of sharks. He kicked them off, and they veered away, but he was nearing exhaustion. Suddenly, he heard the hum of a distant aircraft. He waved his orange life vest and the helicopter crew lowered down a rope ladder to haul him to safety.

Walter had been saved from the jaws of death. We are like Walter Wyatt in that God comes along at the opportune time to snatch us from the jaws of eternal death. We float in despair, fighting off the enemy, and out of nowhere comes our rescue vessel (God) to save the day and our life. What an awesome thing it is to be saved. What an incredible moment when we give it all up to a Savior who cares that we live with Him in eternity, where there will be no despair. All we have to do is call out, "May Day!" and He'll be there in a flash! Go God!

Have you ever felt like it was all over and God saved the day? Has your navigational equipment ever failed you? Take a moment to thank God for saving you from the jaws of eternal death.

DELAYED BROADCAST

Victory in Christ

"In this world you will have trouble, but take heart! I have overcome the world." John 16:33

During a week of vacation in Hawaii, I learned a neat lesson. With the time zone differential, Monday Night Football games are played mid-day in Hawaii. The local TV stations don't air the broadcast until 6:30 p.m. because of prime time billing, but you can find out the result of the game earlier on the radio. Being a die-hard Dallas Cowboy fan (I'm not a fair weather fan either...I was born in Dallas), I couldn't wait until evening to hear the outcome, so I listened to the live broadcast on radio (it just so happened they were playing the Washington Redskins that week). As usual, the Cowboys didn't play great, but they did pull out a squeaker with a last minute field goal to win the game. Later that night I watched the game on TV, even though I already *knew* what the final result was. It didn't matter if the Cowboys fumbled, or threw an interception, or missed an extra point because I knew when all was said and done...my team won!

In our Christian lives, perspective is everything. At times we (fallen, doubtful people) lose our perspective, even though we know what the end result will be. We go through a tough time (trial) in our life and think it's inevitable that we'll lose, so we give up. We lose heart in the midst of the struggle in the game of life and throw in the towel to defeat. Come on, this life we struggle through is nothing but a tape-delayed broadcast in which we (Christians) have already defeated the enemy (opponent), Satan. Guess what? Jesus didn't just pull out the victory in a last ditch effort...He won by a landslide. This game was over before it even started because Jesus is on our team and He is All-Pro. We're on our way to the Super Bowl—heaven! Chalk this one up in the victory column. Life should be more than a dress rehearsal.

Do you ever forget that you are a victor in your walk with Christ? Why is it so easy to give up when things get a little rough? How can we gain a new perspective on trials?

Serving

"If you point these things out to the brothers, you will be a good minister of Christ Jesus, brought up in the truths of faith and of the good teaching that you have followed." 1 Timothy 4:6

In the summer of 1989, Mark Wellman, a paraplegic, gained national recognition by climbing the sheer granite face of "El Capitan" in Yosemite National Park. On the seventh and final day of his heroic climb, the headline of the Fresno newspaper read, "Showing a Will of Granite." Mark's partner, Mike Corbett, who is not paralyzed, received little recognition. With the article was a picture of Mike carrying his companion on his shoulders, subtitled, "Paraplegic and partner prove no wall is too high to scale." The ironic thing about this event is that Mike scaled (climbed) the granite face of El Capitan *three* times in order to help Mark pull himself up once.

You won't find many articles, pictures, broadcasts, or praise going out for a servant. You don't see people flocking around a servant, badgering him for an autograph. To be a servant means to serve when you're not cast in the lead role (the star). Servanthood is a lost art. To *be* a servant is to exemplify humility and selflessness in its truest form (be like Christ). No standing ovations or syndicated TV shows await a humble servant. In fact, servants are looked upon as the lowest member of the food chain. A Doulos (bond-servant) is as low as a snake's belly, seldom recognized, promoted, or viewed very highly by anyone...except God Almighty! God will (not might) exalt you over any mountain (like El Capitan) when you serve others. Serving reveals the Savior. Without it, you'll never accomplish great things for God's Kingdom.

Are you a server or a servee? Do you think serving means giving or getting? Why do you see few Doulos bond-servants in society today? Why do you think Jesus asks you to be one? Will you? Why not?

Faith

"'Have faith in God,' Jesus answered." Mark 11:22

From time to time a lobster (you know the red creatures with clamps for hands) leaves its shell as part of the growth process. The shell means protection, but when the lobster grows, the shell must be abandoned; otherwise, it would soon become a prison, and eventually a casket. The tricky part for the lobster is the period of time between discarding the old shell and forming the new one. During this vulnerable time, the lobster must be scared to death, as the ocean floor currents cartwheel it from coral to kelp. Hungry schools of fish are ready to make it a part of their dinner. For a while at least, the old shell must look pretty good—even if it had begun to feel a little like a girdle. Sometimes the unfortunate lobster dies between shells, but perhaps that's not as bad as suffocating in a shell that no longer fits. So it is with the life of a growing lobster in the ocean blue.

We aren't much different, when it comes to growth. If we didn't have a shell (structure and framework) within which to grow, then I doubt if any of us would have made it this far. Even so, change and growth (maturity) are necessary for survival as a Christian. We don't often see the value at the time of change because it forces us out of our comfort zone and into our faith zone. The only way maturity can take place is to step out into faith and away from security and comfort. Discipleship means being so committed to Jesus that when He asks us to follow Him, to change, to ditch the security and comfort for a ride on faith, to risk it all, to grow, to leave our shells behind and be vulnerable and naked in a tough old world, we answer, "I'm yours, Lord!" Be prepared for anxious (up-tight) moments, fear, doubts, strange looks, and skepticism from others. You know...faith doesn't always make sense, but it doesn't have to.

What is your shell (i.e. comfort zone, security, stronghold)? Why does God call you to leave your shell and become vulnerable? Is that comfortable? Why not? Why are change and maturity two key ingredients to spiritual growth?

A Chain Reaction

Cross

"Pilate had a notice prepared and fastened to the cross. It read: Jesus of Nazareth, King of the Jews." John 19:19

It took place in Los Alamos on May 21, 1946 and it involved a young scientist performing an experiment necessary for testing the atomic bomb in the waters of the south Pacific at Bikini. He'd successfully completed the experiment several times before, but this test would be different. In an effort to determine the amount of U-235 needed for a chain reaction, he would push two hemispheres of uranium together. Then, just at critical mass, he would push them apart with his screwdriver (sounds real hi-tech to me), instantly stopping the chain reaction. As he was about to separate the masses, the screwdriver slipped and the hemispheres of uranium came too close together. Instantly, the room was filled with a bluish haze. Young Louis Slotin reacted and instead of diving for cover and maybe saving himself, he tore the two hemispheres apart bare-handed, thus stopping the chain reaction. By this heroic act, he saved the lives of seven others in the lab, but exposed himself to the dangerous radiation of Uranium 235. Nine days later, he died in agony, but his colleagues survived.

Nineteen centuries ago the Son of the living God walked directly into sin's most concentrated radiation and willingly allowed Himself to be touched by its curse (death). But get this, by this heroic act of courage on the cross, He broke the chain reaction of a sinful world with no hope for a future, and broke the power of sin that began in the laboratory of Eden. He died so that you and I might walk away unharmed into the glory of heaven—what a deal!

What do you feel is the most significant event in the Bible? Why? Is what Christ did on the cross important in your life? Do you see Jesus as a modern day hero, or a forgotten fable?

Sexual Purity

"To the pure, all things are pure." Titus 1:15

The Wall Street Journal reports that in a recent study, one of the reasons the deadly virus HIV causes AIDS is because it is a tenacious opponent. An infected person produces a billion (that's right—billion) particles of the virus *daily*. This is a ton more than anyone had previously believed true. The body's immune system fends off many of these particles, but over time, it's overwhelmed by the attack. The disease's proclivity for mutation has been recognized for quite some time. This, together with the newly discovered productivity, caused a researcher named David Ho (director of the Aaron Diamond AIDS Research Center in New York where HIV's multiplying power was discovered) to state that no drug currently under testing can eradicate the virus in a patient. Even small amounts are capable of eventually producing mutants that can resist any drug. There may be little hope in the medical field, but there is in the spiritual field—purity.

Now, I realize that a percentage of people get this virus through impure blood transfusions, needles, and odd means. I also know, however, that by and large, this deadly disease is transferred through sexual activity. AIDS is not going to be cured by man's hand, but from his heart. Purity is a word seldom heard in casual conversation, but found often in scripture. AIDS is, for the most part, a consequence of immorality. Yes, there are tons of Christians who are cleansed mentally of immorality, but not from its physical consequence. Medical science hasn't created a condom for the conscience yet. Realize that what you do *today* can and will affect your tomorrow. Stop living your life in semesters, thinking that you can play around sexually now, and then settle down when you get older. God's grace is the only cure for this sickness. It starts by purifying our hearts, which leads to purity of our bodies.

Does what you do now affect your future? How? Are you pure? Why does God tell us to live pure and undefiled lives?

Friendship

"For I have no one like him of kindred spirit who will be genuinely concerned for your welfare." Philippians 2:20

Every so often, you run across a person you immediately "mesh" with. So authentic, real, sincere, open, vulnerable, and positive is this person, that you walk away wishing you could have had a little more time with 'em. Somehow you click, a mix of personality and chemistry of thoughts and ideas. How does this happen? Is it mutual interests, common backgrounds, similar personalities, or what? I believe it's more than coincidence. Some people seem to be born with an almost magical, magnetic ability to draw others close to them. What is it? I believe it's open-heartedness, sincere transparency, and unblemished authenticity. Whatever you label it—it involves an ability to accept one's self, accept other people, and humbly open your heart. Somehow, when you meet such a rare breed, you're left with the undeniable impression that "what you saw was what you got." There was no front, camouflage, deceptive label. There was no, "Nice to know ya'," while eyes scanned the room for someone more important than you. I think it was this kind of transparency that made *Forrest Gump* such a successful film. His genuine nature enlisted strangers on benches, befriended fearful soldiers, won over a hard-nosed officer, attracted a blue-eyed blonde, appealed to presidents, and impacted an entire community. Certainly no "normal" person could be so open, simple-hearted, accepting, lacking prejudice or pretense...or could they? Without authenticity, a friendship goes nowhere. It's right at the core of what bonds a friendship. Forrest was real and you should be too.

Are you "real" when you first meet someone? Would anyone describe you as authentic? Do you carry hidden motives and agendas into a conversation? How can you be more "real?"

Tuft Trouble

Straying From God

"Before I was afflicted I went astray, but now I obey your word." Psalms 119:67

Growing up in the great state of Texas, our family did what a lot of folks down there in the Lone Star State do—raise cattle and horses. Today, we no longer do the cattle thing, but we still have about fifty head of horses on a ranch. The reason we stopped raising cattle (other than they are the dumbest creatures on four hooves) is that they get lost all the time. Now, if you were to ask old Carl Ray (my dad), "How come it is that cows get lost and wander off so much?," chances are he would reply, "Well, the cow starts nibbling on a tuft of green grass and when that's gone, it looks ahead to the next tuft, and nibbles on that one. Then it starts nibbling on the tuft next to the hole in the fence, and so on, until the next thing you know, the cow has nibbled itself into being lost." (Read that again with a cowboy accent for maximum effect.)

Americans are in the process of nibbling their way to "lostness." We move from one tuft of activity (or materialism) to another. We never seem to notice just how far off-track we are, or how far away from the truth (Biblical principles) we've managed to wander. When we focus our eyes and thoughts on selfish fulfillment, we lose sight of our spiritual purpose. Being lost effects more than just the one who wanders away, it disrupts those who have to stop what they are doing to search. Yes, God *never* grows weary of looking for the lost (example: prodigal son), but I bet He wishes we would learn from our mistakes. Another scary thing about being lost is that if you get there enough, you'll soon forget what home (being in the will of God) looks like. Do yourself and others around you a huge favor...keep eating, but keep a watchful eye out for where you're headed. Graze on!

What would you describe as a tuft of grass in your life? Does it ever cause you to get lost spiritually? How long does it take you to realize this? What do you do to get back on track?

Mom

Parenting

"Her children arise up and call her blessed, her husband also, and he prizes her." Proverbs 31:28

"Her ability to love is exceeded only by God's love itself." Rex Burns

"All that I am or hope to be, I owe to my angel mother." Abraham Lincoln

"It's at our mother's knee that we acquire our noblest and truest and highest ideals." Mark Twain

The love of a mother is *never* exhausted, it never changes, and it never tires. Our society has placed a demeaning connotation on the title of housewife and mom. What people tend to forget is that it's a mother that makes a house a home. Career seems to have edged out the most important job on this earth, mothering a child. I need a little room on this page to flat out brag on my wife, who is the greatest mother to my three boys. My sons worship the precious ground she walks on. Why? Because she cares like God cares for them. No, she's not perfect by any means, but you'll have a heck of a time convincing my boys she's not. When God created the female, He personally installed in their chassis a gift for nurturing that seems to work on auto-pilot all day, every day. There is no greater responsibility or job, yesterday, today, or in our hi-tech future, that equals motherhood. I try (as a father), but I can't hold a candle to my wife when it comes to raising God-fearing children. She soothes with her voice, she hugs with her breast, and she loves with her heart.

No matter what you might think of your mom, realize this—she's the only mom you'll ever have. Respect your mom, honor your mom, care for your mom, protect your mom, pray for your mom, encourage your mom, and lastly...value her.

Go right now, no matter where she is, and tell your mom you love her. Write her a love note, give her a hug, serve her, make her breakfast in bed, do your chores without being told. Tonight, hit your knees and pray for your mom and the mom you want to be or marry.

GET READY

Christian Journey

"Be ye therefore ready also." Luke 12:40

One of the greatest needs today is to be a Christian ready to face Christ at any turn. This is about as easy as eating soup with a fork. The biggest battle in our journey is not against sin, difficulties, or circumstances, but against being so wrapped up in what we do in our daily trek that we aren't ready to face Christ around the next corner. Our one great need is not for a defining creed, or figuring out if we are of any value to God, but to be ready to face Him. The funny (mostly scary) thing about this subject is that Jesus rarely comes when or where we expect. Rather, we find Him when we *least* expect—kind of a surprise attack, and always in the most illogical situations and circumstances. The only way a believer can keep true to our Lord is by being ready for His surprise visits. It's not what we are doing, but who we are in the deep closets of our soul that is important. He wants our life to reflect the attitude of child-wonder. If we honestly want to "be ready" for Jesus, we must stop being religious, and be spiritually sincere. Our culture will stereotype you as impractical and dreamy if you live out a life of "looking off to Jesus," but when He does appear in the midst of a trial, or when the heat is turned up in your life, you will be the only one who is ready. Don't trust, obey, follow, or listen to anyone, even the finest saint who ever walked this planet, if they hinder your sight of Christ. Get ready today, don't wait for tomorrow...it could be too late.

If Christ were to come today, this very minute, would you be ready? What do you need to do to get yourself ready? What does "ready" mean? Describe who you know that you feel is ready.

Movies

"Your eyes will see strange things, and your mind will utter perverse things." Proverbs 23:33

Summertime is definitely the bread-and-butter of Hollywood. According to *Movieguide* magazine there is a little different twist to the reports coming out of movie land. Despite Hollywood's insistence that it is making more movies for the American family, less than half of 1994's releases were rated acceptable for teenagers or for children. The report went something like this:

NC-17 rated movies	1%
G rated movies	3%
Not rated movies	14%
PG rated movies	19%
PG-13 rated movies	22%
R rated movies	41%

Now, there is no one who loves a good flick (movie) more than me. Buttered popcorn, 32 ounce soda pop, Junior Mints, and Gummy Bears are as mandatory at a movie as hot dogs and soft pretzels are at a baseball game. The problem is the standards of the movie rating system. Violence, sex, and offensive language are huge box office draws. You can't tell me you can watch a two hour movie infected with nudity (or sexual connotations), excessive violence, and offensive language, and not be swayed by these brain-branding scenes. These impure movies are easily accessed at theaters, in hotel rooms, or on your home TV set. Whether you see it or not, your character, beliefs, standards, and rationale is persuaded to agree with Hollywood's philosophies. Every time you buy a movie ticket, you are supporting the production of another movie. My plea to you is send a message to movie-land, loud and clear, that you are not (as a Christian) going to lower your integrity or standards to this filth any longer. You can't turn off your mind or shut your ears, so flee (run or avoid) from this junk. Next time you're watching a movie, ask yourself if Jesus were to appear in physical form next to you, would you still watch it?

What rating do you go to? R? PG-13? Are PG movies free of sex, violence, or offensive language? Are the movies you watch acceptable by Jesus' standards?

Forgiveness

"There is forgiveness with Thee." Psalms 130:4

It's like a steel trap that snares its victims with little hope for release. Your mind and your memory can either provide freedom, or lock you in an emotional prison. Chuck Swindoll said, "Life is 10% what happens and 90% how you react to what happens." That's the key. Okay, so you don't deck someone for treating you unfairly, or practice tit-for-tat strategies either. No so fast though! Retaliation will often take a more subtle form. The best way to ensure true forgiveness is to be aware of the sly ways people *don't* forgive each other, like:

Gossip—We make negative reports about someone else, driving a wedge.

Criticism (without constructive advice)—We complain and nag the people who offend us until they are as hurt as we think we are.

Withdrawal—We avoid, deprive, or exclude from our plans and company those people who hurt us.

Self-appointed martyrdom—Using a real or imagined injury, we manipulate people into feeling sorry for us.

Constructive criticism—While helpful criticism encourages and corrects, even good advice becomes "poison" when it's motivated by disappointment and resentment.

Humility is the key to this whole forgiveness issue. Phillips Brooks wrote, "The true way to be humble is not to stoop until you are smaller than yourself, but to stand at your real height against some higher nature that will show you what the real smallness of your greatness is." Forgive and forget...it's the ultimate in abundant living and freedom.

Are you a forgiving person? Do you feel that you have any bitterness towards anyone? Do you forget easily? Do you hold grudges?

GROWTH CHART

Comparison

"I planted, Apollos watered, but God causes the growth." 1 Corinthians 3:6

Growing up can be one of the most fun experiences in life. Three sons fill our house with wrestling, war, GI Joe's, monster grocery lists, scabby knees, dirty clothes, and intense competition—you can imagine the total chaos. We measure the boys each month on a growth chart attached to the wall. One day, the chart slipped from the wall and my oldest son, Daniel, tried to re-hang it. As he did, the chart slipped off the nail and rested flush with the floor...about four inches short of the original height. Daniel got his brother, Dustin, up against the chart the next day, then came running into the room yelling, "Mommy! Mommy! Dustin grew four inches this month." My wife responded, "That's impossible, he's only two years old. Let's go see." They walked up to the bedroom, where suspicions were confirmed—the chart was set at an improper height.

We can easily repeat Daniel's mistake in gauging our spiritual growth. Compared to a shortened scale, we may appear better than we are, or more mature in Christ. It is only when we stand against the cross, that "great leveler of men" (as A.T. Robertson called it), that we cannot think of ourselves more highly than we should. Jesus must be the standard against which we measure ourselves. When we stand against friends or society we elevate our spiritual mentality. Match up with Christ and you'll remain focused and on track. Growth is a slow, steady, daily process that takes time and effort through Christ to accomplish.

Do you compare yourself to others? To what is standard do you compare yourself? How do you match up? What is the danger of comparing yourself to worldly standards?

Commitment

"For now we really live if we stand firm in the Lord." 1 Thessalonians 3:8

This is a story about a home church in the Soviet Union that received one copy of the Gospel of Luke, the only scripture most of these Christians had ever seen. They tore it into small sections and gave out the pieces to the body of believers. The plan was to memorize the portion, then on the next Lord's Day, meet and redistribute the scriptural sections. On Sunday the church-goers arrived at the house church inconspicuously, in small groups throughout the day, so as not to arouse the suspicion of KGB informers. By dusk they were all safely inside and began singing hymns quietly, but with sincere worship. Suddenly, the door flew open and in walked two soldiers with loaded guns. One soldier shouted, "All right, everybody line up against the wall. If you wish to renounce your commitment to Jesus Christ, leave now!" Two or three quickly left, then another. "This is your last chance to either stay and die or leave safely." A few more slipped out into the darkness while parents and children trembled in fear. After a few moments of silence, the other soldier closed the door, looked back at those who remained, and said, "Keep your hands up, but this time in praise to our Lord Jesus Christ, brothers and sisters. We, too, are Christians. We were sent to another house church several weeks ago to arrest a group of believers, but instead we were converted. We have learned, however, that unless people are willing to die for their faith, they cannot be trusted."

Our commitment to Christ affects every other relationship we have. The deeper our devotion and commitment to Christ, the more faithful we are to our spouse, family, church, job, friends, and people we come in contact with. Stand firm in your faith to Christ!

How important is your faith to you? Are you committed? What could cause you to flee?

The Moe Color The Moe Better

Racism

"If someone says, 'I love God,' and hates his brother, he is a liar; for the one who does not love his brother whom he has seen, cannot love God whom he has not seen." 1 John 4:20

I realize that this is the second devotional I've included on this topic. I don't mean to beat a dead horse (figure of speech), but this is a sensitive, highly volatile subject. You can interchange words easily—prejudice, discrimination, hostility, bias, partiality, racism, bigotry, or whatever. Webster's (you know, that thick book you'd just as soon not use) defines racism as the belief that race is the primary determinant of human traits and capacities and that racial differences produce an inherent superiority of a particular race. We operate under the false pretense that our race, whether it be African American, Anglo-Saxon, Asian, Hispanic, or another tribe, people, or nation, is better or more elite than another. Now, I realize writing a devotional on this touchy subject is *not* gonna' solve the racial tension we have in this world, *but* conviction through impacted scripture can change hearts. A good friend of mine saw a picture of two young boys returning from a fishing trip, walking down a dusty country road, arms around each other...one black, one white. The caption under the picture was, "The more color, the more better."

This world has always had folks who are prejudiced, but you and I don't have to join in on stupidity and ignorant thinking. Your brother is anyone you come in contact with (it doesn't mean literal kin) and you are to love them for being created by God, loved by God, directed by God, as a child of God. There is no racial superiority on this earth, because we *all* are sinners (losers) who need a Savior. Cultivate new friendships outside your race, find value in not going with the flow. Prove the love of Christ in your heart and love your brother no matter what color his skin is. Remember... "Moe Color, Moe Better!"

How do you feel about other races? Do you have friends of other races? Do you laugh at racial jokes or use racial slamming, stereotype words? Do you love your brother no matter what his color?

Jesus

"There is no Savior besides me." Isaiah 43:11

The sun had just risen over the small village of Plelo in German-occupied France on a hot summer day in 1944. A fifteen-year-old boy didn't understand why he and his community had been brought before a firing squad in the town square. Maybe it was because they had hidden out from a unit of Marquisards (French underground freedom fighters), or perhaps merely to satisfy the blood-thirsty German commander's need for revenge. No matter the reason, they knew they were about to die. As the young boy stood in front of the firing squad, memories of childhood began to pop into his mind—running around the French countryside, playing in the streets, kick-ball games. Most of all, he feared the feeling of bullets entering his body. He hoped no one would see his tears or hear his cries, so he exhaled and closed his eyes. Suddenly, he heard exploding mortar behind the building, tanks rolling into town. The German firing squad ran for cover and the boy saw a unit of US tanks led by Bob Hamsley. After three hours, fifty Nazis were dead and another fifty were taken prisoner. In 1990 the town of Plelo honored Captain Hamsley on the very spot (town square) where dozens of village residents were nearly executed. The man who initiated the search for Hamsley and the ceremony honoring him was the former fifteen-year-old boy. He was determined to find the man who saved his life and honor him.

This is a touching story about remembering and honoring a savior. What a neat testimony of a man who was indebted to a savior (Captain Hamsley) and refused to go through life without recognizing him. Never forget the Savior (Jesus) who rescued you.

Do you forget your Savior? Why? How can you honor Him? Will you? How? When?

CAMEL KNEES

Prayer

"I say to you, love your enemies and pray for those who persecute you." Matthew 5:44

According to an Associatied Press release in September 1994, Cindy Hartman of the metropolis of Conway, Arkansas, walked into her house to answer the phone and was confronted by a burglar. He ripped the phone line out of the wall and ordered her into a closet at gun-point. Cindy immediately dropped to her knees and asked the thief if she could pray for him. "I want you to know that God loves you and I forgive you," she said. The thief apologized for what he had done and then yelled to a woman waiting in a pick-up outside, "We've got to unload all of this. This is a Christian home and a Christian family. We can't do this to them." As Cindy remained on her knees, the thief returned all the furniture he had stolen, then took the bullets from the gun, handed it to her, and walk out the door.

James, the half brother who only accepted Jesus for who He was after the resurrection, was referred to as "Camel Knees." Why? Because camels' knees are callused from spending so much time kneeling on them. Praying for the enemy is not only incredibly disarming, but seldom done. What an awesome testimony of faith it would be if we, as a body of Christ, would pray for those who are out to destroy us. It is easy to pray for family and friends, but how about an enemy? An enemy is one who harbors hatred and malicious intent toward you, or someone who directly opposes you or your cause. Enemies need your prayers...badly.

When did you last pray for someone you hate? Why? Who do you pray for most often? Why does Jesus tell us to pray for those who want to harm us?

Giving

"Each man should give what he has decided in his heart to give, not reluctantly or under compulsion, for God loves a cheerful giver." 2 Corinthians 9:7

Birds of the air are interesting to watch. Now, I don't I consider myself a real bird watcher, but you can learn a lot from them. There is a lesson in watching the swallow teach its young to fly. The mother bird gets the chicks out of the nest, high atop a tree, and starts shoving them out toward the end of the branch. Before the chicks do a nose-dive into the pavement, they learn to fly. If a chick tightens its talons (claws) on the branch and refuses to jump, the mother will peck at its feet. When the chick can't stand the pain anymore, it lets go and flies. Birds have feet and can walk, talons that can grasp a tree branch tightly, but flying is their heritage. Not until they fly are they living at their best and doing what they were intended to do.

You know, giving is what Christians do best. It is the air into which we were born. It is the action that was designed into us before our birth, yet sometimes we desperately try to hold on and live for self. We look bedraggled and pathetic doing it, hanging on to the dead branch of a bank account, afraid to risk ourselves on the untried wings of giving. We don't think we can live generously because we've never tried it before. The sooner we start, the quicker we find the joy that accompanies giving and letting go for God. God will peck at the closed hands of our heart until we stop feeling, or let go and let God. Flying is more fun than watching anyway.

Are you a giver? To what do you give? Are you a horder? Why? Did you come into this world with money? Are you gonna' leave this world with money? How can you become a better giver?

Being Thankful

"Let the peace of Christ rule in your hearts, to which indeed you were called in one body; and be thankful." Colossians 3:15

Mother Theresa, one of the most Godly women to roam this planet, told this story in an address to the National Prayer Breakfast. In a foreign country one evening, she went out and picked up four people from off the streets (bums). One of the four was in sad shape, so she told the other three, "I will take care of the one in the worst condition." Mother Theresa did for her all that her love could do. She put her in a warm bed and there was a smile on her face as she did so. The sick woman took her hand and said only two words, "Thank you," and then she died. Mother Teresa addressed the group, "I couldn't help but examine my conscience before her. I asked myself what would I say if I were in her place? My answer was simple. I would have said I'm hungry, dying, and in pain. She gave me much more than I gave her (a bed), she gave me her grateful love and died with a smile on her face."

Isn't it ironic that gratitude brings a smile to people and becomes such a wonderful gift? Mother Theresa has such a neat perspective and wonderful outlook on life. God puts you in situations daily where you can take the honors or give the glory to Him—your choice. To be grateful means to appreciate the kindness and grace you have been given or shown. Calvary (the cross) is a supreme (and we're not talking pizza) example of gratitude. Be thankful for every day you live and all the many blessings which come standard with each day.

For what or whom are you thankful? What does gratitude mean to you? Are you one of those who takes things for granted? Why? How can you be grateful for all you have? Will you? When? How?

Contentment

"Not that I speak from want; for I have learned to be content in whatever circumstance I am in." Philippians 4:11

I once rented a movie I thought would be a total flop. I was wrong. *Cool Runnings* was about a Jamaican bobsled team training for the Olympics (like they've got snow in Jamaica). John Candy, now deceased, played a former American gold medalist who coached this joke of a team. The team members grew to like their coach and called him the "sled-god." Later in the movie, the coach's dark history came out. In the Olympics, following his gold medal performance, he broke the rules by weighting the US sled, bringing disgrace on himself, the team, and America. One of the Jamaican bobsledders couldn't quite understand why anyone who had already won a gold medal would cheat. The coach replied, "I had to win. I learned something though. If you aren't happy without a gold medal, you won't be happy with one either."

To be satisfied by who we are and what we have is a rare thing. Most of us want a bigger house, nicer car, fatter bank account, better weather, younger look, smoother talk, more satisfying relationship, and more comfortable life. We get frustrated when our path is blocked by a trial or unusual circumstance that causes us to step back and see what is *really* important in life. You, yes you, will learn which mountains in life you must climb. You can't climb them all, so you have to prioritize. The older and grayer you get, the more you find out that what's important isn't places, circumstances, or things, but faith, family, and friends.

What satisfies you best? Are you a content person? Why not? What would make you content? Is contentment a place you arrive, or an attitude between your ears?

Discipleship

"Which one of you, when he builds a tower, doesn't first sit down and calculate the cost." Luke 14:28

"Make my day!" "Feel lucky?" "Dying ain't easy, boy." Okay, a little trivia for you. Who said these famous words? If your answer was Hillary Clinton, you're a bonehead. If you said Clint Eastwood you win a new car! (Just kidding.) In the film, *In the Line of Fire,* Clint played a Secret Service agent named Frank Horrigan. Horrigan had protected the life of the President for more than three decades, but was haunted by the memory of what happened thirty years before. Horrigan was a young agent assigned to President Kennedy on that fateful day in Dallas in 1963. When the assassin fired, Horrigan froze in shock. Thirty years later he wrestled with the question of whether he could take a bullet for the President.

You know a great question to ask yourself is who would you die for? A Secret Service Agent is sworn to loyalty, no matter what the cost. You don't sign up to be a Secret Service Agent and go through years of training unless you can commit to a cause that could ultimately cost you your life. You, as a Christian, need to count the cost of being a disciple before you enlist. We must be willing to jump in front of persecution, false accusations, dishonesty, and evil for the cause of Christ. We are to protect our Savior at all times, at all cost. We should be willing to stand up for a higher cause on a moment's notice, not freeze in shock. Protecting the President of the United States is a big deal, but not nearly the commitment that's needed to be a disciple for Christ.

Who are you willing to "take a bullet for?" Are you a Secret Service Agent for the cause of Christ? How do you protect Christ? When? When do you freeze?

God's Power Plant

God's Power

"I will instruct you in the power of God." Job 27:11

The process is amazing when you see it all at work. Huge shovels dig house-size scoops of lignite coal. Pulverized and loaded onto railroad box cars, the coal travels to a generating plant in east Texas, where it is further crushed into powder. Super-heated, this powder ignites like gasoline when blown into huge furnaces that crank three turbines. Whirring at 3,600 rpm, these turbines are housed in concrete and steel casings one hundred feet long, ten feet tall, and ten feet across. They generate enough electricity for thousands of people. A visitor to this plant once asked the chief engineer where the electricity was stored. The answer was, "We don't store it, we just make it." When a light switch is flipped a hundred miles away, it places a demand on the system and prompts greater output.

Not that you are interested in power plants or their usage, but I think it makes a great point of how God's power cannot be stored up either. Though inexhaustible, it comes in the measure required at the moment needed. God's power has a way of not overloading our circuits and causing a thermal melt-down, but being just enough. God's almighty power is not to be concealed or unused. It is to be a source of stabilization and divine energy that comes to us at the flip of a spiritual switch. God intended us to access this source through His Spirit. There are no forms to fill out, no waiting list, and no bill at the end of the month...just flip it on and use it up, for His Glory and Praise, Amen!

How powerful is God's grace? When are we to use it? How does He supply us that power we need at an exact moment? Do you tap into it often? Why or why not?

Divine Donor

Cross

"While we (you) were yet sinners (about to die) Christ died for us (you)." Romans 5:8

National Geographic has always been an interesting magazine to me. It is filled with literature and pictures (I like those the most) of places on this planet I'll probably never see, and most I never knew existed. In the September 1991 issue, an article tells of a young man from Hanover, Pennsylvania (like I said, places I've never heard of) who was severely burned in a boiler explosion. To save his life, the doctors covered him with six thousand square centimeters of donated skin, as well as sheets of skin cultured from a stamp-sized piece of his own unburned skin. A reporter from the magazine asked him, "Do you ever think about the donor who saved you?" The young man replied, "To be alive because of a dead donor is too big, too much, so I don't think about it."

Christians have received a similar gift from God—Jesus. It is overwhelming, but it is worth thinking about. The cross was and still is a great example of God filling out a donor card so that we might live, at the expense of His only Son. If we could only catch a glimpse of the sacrificial event on Calvary, we'd blow a fuse. I don't think we mean to, but we have a tendency to take for granted just how awesome (there's that word again) the cross is in our lives. We would have no hope, joy, peace, future, or reason to get out of bed without it. Take a moment today, apart from your busy agenda, and ponder how He died for you so that you might live for Him. Go ahead, ponder with me, won't you?

Take the next ten minutes and think about what Jesus did for you on the cross of Calvary between two thieves.

Sacrifice

"Even if I am being poured out as a drink offering upon the sacrifice and service of your faith." Philippians 2:17

Father Maximilian Kolbe was a prisoner at Auschwitz in August, 1941. Another prisoner escaped from the camp, and in reprisal, the Nazis ordered ten prisoners to die by starvation. Father Kolbe offered to take the place of one of the condemned men. The Nazis kept Kolbe in the starvation bunker for two solid weeks and then put him to death by lethal injection on August 14, 1941. Thirty years later, a survivor of Aushwitz described the effect of Father Kolbe's sacrificial action:

It was an enormous shock to the whole camp. We realized that someone among us in the spiritual dark night of the soul was raising the standard of life on high. Someone unknown, like everyone else, tortured and bereft of name and social standing, went to a horrible death for the sake of someone not even related to him. Therefore it is not true, we cried, that humanity is cast down and trampled in the mud, overcome by oppressors, and overwhelmed by hopelessness. Thousands of prisoners were convinced the true world continued to exist and that our torturers would not be able to destroy it. To say that Father Kolbe died for us or for that person's family is too great a simplification. His death was the salvation of thousands.... We were stunned by his act, which became for us a mighty explosion of light in the dark camp.

What an incredible story of self-denial. How our world marvels at such an act of sacrifice. What an impact it would make on you and I to exemplify such sacrificial love for those with whom we have *no* relation. Jesus started the way for us to follow. It's easy to sacrifice for those we love, but how about those we don't care for, or don't even know? Sacrifice with *no* recognition is only done by divine intervention.

What is the biggest sacrifice you ever made? When did you do this? What does hecatomb mean? (Look it up.) What is the greatest example of sacrifice you've ever seen or heard of?

Family

"Do not be deceived, God is not mocked; for whatever a man sows, this he will also reap." Galatians 6:7

What began in 1990 as the dream of Bill McCartney, former head coach of the University of Colorado Buffaloes football team, is today the fastest growing men's movement in the United States. Coach "Mac," who led his team to the national title in college football, resigned his $325,000 a year job to practice what he preached, and devote his full time and attention to his wife, kids, and the Promise Keepers' movement. Prior to this radical move, his life had been a blur of off-season recruiting, late afternoon practices, and weekend college road trips, with little time for his family. Coach Mac was led by his commitment to Christ to gather seventy men together for the purpose of encouragement and support in their roles as husbands and fathers. Today, supporters number in the hundreds of thousands, packing stadiums in major cities each year. This movement calls men of integrity back to their responsibility without encouraging a harsh, authoritarian leadership. Commitment to the family should not be one of control, but of research and development.

Of late, the family has been spiritually led by the woman. Our society needs to see what spiritual men, as husbands and fathers committed to Christ, look like. The Promise Keepers' movement is an attempt (it's working) to reverse this trend and encourage men to be involved at home with their time and spiritual input.

What does this movement mean to you today? Tons! You can start now to develop the qualities necessary to be a Promise Keeper. You won't just wake up transformed, or take a magic pill that turns you into a committed man of integrity and conviction. Don't think for one minute that what you are doing won't effect your tomorrow. It will! The choices and decisions you make now will in turn make you later. Be a man of your word; be a leader through Christ; be a man of high values; be consistent with your talk and walk. Be all you can be! You will reap what you sow. Be a Promise Keeper.

Write down five goals you wish to attain in five years. How do plan to attain them? When do you start pursuing?

Topical Index